The IRA and Retirement Plan Owner's Guide to

Beating *the* New Death Tax

6 Proven Strategies to Protect Your Family from The SECURE Act

James Lange, CPA/Attorney

Lange Financial Group, LLC
2200 Murray Avenue
Pittsburgh, PA 15217
412.521.2732
admin@paytaxeslater.com

Manufactured by Maple Press, *York, PA*

Book Cover & Interior Layout by Abrams Design, *Pittsburgh, PA*

Cartoons by Randy Bish, *Greensburg, PA*

Effective January 1, 2020

The SECURE Act Will Extract a Devastating Tax from Families of IRA and Retirement Plan Owners...

But it Doesn't Have to be that Way.

Inside: Safe, Easy, and 100% Legal Ways after the SECURE Act, COVID-19 and the CARES Act to Keep Your Legacy Wealth in Your Family's Hands ... and Out of Uncle Sam's ... Without Raising an Eyebrow at the IRS.

Dear IRA and/or Retirement Plan Owner and Hopefully New Friend:

To oversimplify, the SECURE Act—a new tax bill that went into effect and became law on January 1, 2020—forces our heirs to suffer massive income tax acceleration on inherited IRAs and retirement plans within ten years of the IRA owner's death. Granted there are some exceptions, including spouses, but it will have potentially devastating effects on the hard-earned wealth in your IRA and other retirement accounts.

I find this tax change particularly infuriating. It's almost as if Congress were sitting around thinking "What group could we hurt the most? How about taxpayers who pursued the American dream and worked hard for 30 or 40 years and played by the rules?" You dutifully sacrificed and put as much money as possible in your IRAs and retirement plan. They told you putting money in your IRA and retirement plan was great for you and your kids. Now, late in the game, after relying on their representations, they pull the rug right out from under you. Now, they are attempting to confiscate a third of your IRA or retirement plan after you die.

Don't accept this. Fight back and protect your family.

You made a wise choice buying this book. Now that it is in your hands, I urge you to read the Overview of the book which begins on page 1. Please also look at the detailed Table of Contents and read the chapters or sections that interest you the most. Roth IRA conversions have taken on a new urgency as a consequence of COVID-19 and the Coronavirus Aid, Relief, and Economic Security Act (CARES). You will likely enjoy significant benefits by reading Chapter 6.

Don't skip Chapter 8. There is a giant loophole in the Setting Every Community Up for Retirement Enhancement Act (SECURE Act) that might be a great solution for you: charitable remainder trusts (CRTs) as the beneficiary of your IRA. Chapter 8 has the details. To oversimplify, given certain reasonable assumptions, if you explicitly leave a million-dollar IRA to your child (or children), your child runs out of money at age 81. If you leave that same million dollars to a charitable remainder trust with your child as the income beneficiary, with your child spending the same amount of money, your child will still have $465,175 at 81 and the charity will get $452,211.

It is great for your child, great for the charity … and the big loser is the IRS.

When we discovered how beneficial this strategy was to many reader's children, and potentially your children, it became our goal to help direct a billion dollars to charity. We only need a small percentage of IRA millionaires who are a good fit for this solution to act on this idea to reach our goal; but our first goal is your safety and security, then your children's safety and security. The fact that charities get money at the end is a huge bonus, but not our primary objective.

Obviously, we would be thrilled if you read the entire book. It might take a couple of hours, but the strategies could save you and your heirs literally hundreds of thousands of dollars, sometimes more.

The federal government calls it the SECURE Act. But as a CPA, attorney, and investment advisor for 3+ decades, I believe a much more appropriate name for the new tax bill would be…

"The Extreme Death-Tax for IRA and Retirement Plan Owners Act"

That's because the new SECURE Act greatly accelerates the rate at which the legacy wealth in your IRA is taxed once you are gone and your heirs inherit it.

The bottom line: This onerous change in the tax laws now enables the IRS to confiscate as much as ONE-THIRD of the money in your IRA and retirement plans.

Then, right after the passage of the SECURE Act comes COVID-19. The double whammy could financially decimate your legacy and that of millions of other Americans who have worked so hard and sacrificed to accumulate IRAs. Congress put the screws to us with the SECURE Act and who do you think is going to pay for COVID-19 and the CARES Act? If you do nothing, it will probably be you and your family and families like yours. The tax reduction strategies recommended in this book take on a new urgency after COVID-19. We should not take this fate lying down. And we are all in this together.

One piece of relief that we cover in the book is the Coronavirus Aid, Relief, and Economic Security Act (CARES).

We do not cover the bill as a stand-alone topic, but rather interweave the different opportunities the bill creates for IRA and retirement plan owners.

I wrote this book to help you legally FIGHT BACK against the unmitigated gall and greed of the federal government … enabling you to keep your wealth in your family's hands, and out of Uncle Sam's greedy paws.

In these pages, you discover tested strategies that protect your wealth against the outright pillaging of your IRA that the SECURE Act otherwise permits. The book covers all of the following and much more:

- How to use Roth conversions to minimize taxes on your IRA income for decades—for both you and your family. Again, Roth IRA conversions are particularly urgent with the arrival of COVID-19 and the CARES Act.
- How to optimize Social Security strategies in light of the SECURE Act.
- Gifting strategies for adroitly maximizing family wealth under the SECURE Act.
- Updating your wills and trusts for greater flexibility and protection against the SECURE Act.
- How to ensure financial security for your surviving spouse after you pass.
- Why leaving your IRA to a charitable remainder trust (CRT) can be more beneficial to your children than leaving the IRA to them outright—as bizarre as that may sound.
- Placing each of your assets in the optimal type of account to reduce your taxes both now and after you pass.
- Why owning investments in jointly held accounts with your spouse is probably a bad idea after the SECURE Act.
- Combining multiple tax-reduction methods for maximum benefit.
- Tax-loss harvesting after COVID-19.
- And more.

After reading this book, you may have questions about how these tax-reducing and investment strategies work. Or perhaps you might like us to develop your personal financial masterplan and implement it for you.

If you are interested in getting our help, please turn to page 175 to see if it makes sense for us to talk.

Sincerely,

James Lange, CPA/Attorney

P.S. We have a special bonus for purchasers of this book. In February 2020, we held an all-day live in person workshop on how to legally *prevent* the New Death Tax from accelerating and increasing taxes on your legacy wealth. However, as we go to press, the coronavirus has made public gatherings too risky for the foreseeable future. The good news is that we videotaped that all-day workshop held in February 2020.

There was a certain energy in that workshop between me and the 90 participants that I can't replicate with a webinar. That energy comes through on the video making it more enjoyable to watch and easier to hold your attention.

I want you to have the benefits of that workshop. It was up to date in February, and I added a special COVID-19 update on how IRA and retirement plan owners can take advantage of the opportunities offered by the Coronavirus Aid, Relief, and Economic Security Act (CARES).

Of course, there is considerable overlap between the information in the presentation and the book, but some material is different. I cannot stress too strongly the advantages of seeing and hearing ideas as well as reading about them—studies have proven that covering material more than once through multiple types of input reinforces and supports better learning and will give you more confidence to take action. And frankly, this material is well worth your valuable time.

You can watch the video either on your computer or your television in the comfort and privacy of your own home—no need to risk leaving your home and sit with other attendees.

To claim your free *Retire Secure* DVD, call **1-800-387-1129** today. Or complete and mail or fax (**412-521-2285**) the reply form on the last page of this book now. You'll be glad you did.

P.P.S. *We are contributing 100% of the gross proceeds of the book sales and royalties to* **charity: water,** *a charity dedicated to bringing potable drinking water to people in developing countries.*

Praise for:

The IRA and Retirement Plan Owner's Guide to
Beating the New Death Tax:

6 Proven Strategies to Protect Your Family from The SECURE Act

"Minimization of costs and taxes are the key elements of every financial plan. On the tax front, there is no one better than Jim Lange to provide timely and useful bedrock tax solutions."

> — **Burton G. Malkiel,**
> Author, *A Random Walk Down Wall Street*, 12th ed. 2019

"Jim Lange has packed an astounding amount of information and warnings on how The SECURE Act will negatively impact unsuspecting clients—and clear and practical suggestions for how to deal with this stealth tax in his book. The book is a quick read but is an incredible time-saving research resource for professionals who want to help defer the impact of this accelerated tax attack. Don't underestimate the draconian devastation that this murder of the "stretch IRA" could cost IRA and retirement plan inheritors—possibly up to 1/3rd of the money in their accounts! Jim's experience and wisdom will guide you through several big money-saving game plan scenarios."

> — **Stephan R. Leimberg, Esq.,**
> Publisher, **Leimberg Information Services, Inc. (LISI)**

"Jim has once again done a brilliant job in making a complicated topic easy to understand. There is no doubt in my mind that any IRA or retirement account owner can save tens or even hundreds of thousands of dollars in unnecessary taxes by employing some or all of the strategies presented."

> — **Bill Losey, CFP®**
> **Bill Losey Retirement Solutions**

"James Lange's book on *Beating the New Death Tax* is a necessary read and raises the focus on how current legislation continues to punish retirees and those who have been playing "by the rules" in planning for retirement. Just as we've seen Medicare rules impact those who have saved for retirement, Lange's book reveals that "doing the right thing" and saving for retirement and protecting your heirs will land you right in the "cross hairs" of the tax man and government regulators. Fortunately, Lange reveals how to address this situation and protect your nest egg and that of your heirs with valuable and actionable advice in this must-read book."

— **Jack Tatar,** Author,
Having the Talk: The Four Keys to Your Parents' Safe Retirement

"This is a powerful, practical book that arms you with the strategies you need to save or make yourself thousands of dollars!"

— **Brian Tracy,** Author, Speaker, Consultant,
Brian Tracy International

"James Lange's book, *The Retirement Plan Owner's Guide to Beating the New Death Tax,* is a valuable resource with sensible information and practice planning strategies that can be easily put into practice. This book will be very helpful and is a must for both taxpayers and their advisors."

— **Robert S. Keebler,** CPA/PFS, MST, AEP *(Distinguished)*

"*The IRA and Retirement Plan Owner's Guide to Beating the New Death Tax* is a straightforward read for the do-it-yourself investor/financial planner/tax preparer. For those readers who like to collaborate with their team of various advisors, this will also be beneficial.

As with previous books, Jim lays out impactful, financially significant ideas for you to consider, and potentially implement. Jim takes the COVID-19 crisis with portfolios declining into account and recommends strategies investors can take now.

Finally, many of these ideas prompt legacy conversations with loved ones, which hopefully lead to tightening family bonds, especially in times of fear, worry, and the never-ending creep of screen time and social media influencers."

— **Adam Yofan,** Wealth Advisor, **Buckingham Strategic Wealth**

"Jim Lange's latest book, *The IRA and Retirement Plan Owner's Guide to Beating the New Death Tax*, is another "must read" from Jim's experienced tax-saving pen. Jim clearly explains the problems generated by passage of The SECURE Act in order to illustrate his clear and exceptional solutions to these challenges.

If you have been a long-time reader of Jim's many books and a follower of his learned advice, you will be comfortable and can rest at ease with Jim's guidance to save yourself and family members from this scary legislation.

Byzantine and complicated topics such as: *"Death of the Lifetime Stretch" 10-Year Provision, "Enhancements" for IRAs, RMD Age Change Requirements, "Back-Door" Roth IRA Contributions, Roth IRA Conversions, Social Security Planning, Estate Planning, Gifting, and Charitable Remainder Trusts (CRT)* are detailed and explained clearly by Jim through his customized process and seasoned delivery style.

Don't let your guard down...listen to Jim's valuable advice...it could potentially save you 10's or even 100's of thousands of dollars in taxes over your and your children's lifetime."

— **P. J. DiNuzzo, CPA/CFP,**
Author, *The Seven Keys to Investing Success*

"Few advisors are as knowledgeable about IRAs and retirement plans as Jim Lange. Through the use of real-world questions and answers, examples and illustrations, this book delivers critical and timely strategies that could save the families of IRA and retirement plan owners hundreds of thousands of dollars."

— **Nicole L. Maholtz**, President and CEO,
Brentmark Software, *(Top IRA software trusted by most IRA experts)*

"I have constantly maintained that using even one tax planning idea can save people thousands. Jim Lange's book, *The Retirement Plan Owner's Guide to Beating the New Death Tax*, is a fantastic resource loaded with many gems that could save clients a bundle. It is clearly written and has great insight into the SECURE Act that should make this book a MUST read for all IRA owners, financial planners and tax professionals."

— **Sandy Botkin, CPA Esq.,**
Author, *Lower Your Taxes Big Time* and Tax Director,
Expense Tracking Application, TAXBOT

"This is simple: if you have a large IRA, you need to learn how The SECURE Act killed the IRA Stretch—and what to do about it. Read Jim Lange's new book, *The Retirement Plan Owner's Guide to Beating the New Death Tax*. My favorite chapters are Chapters 2, 3 and 8. Why? They will help you protect your children's inheritance."

> — **Julie Jason**,
> Author, *Retire Securely* and *The Retirement Survival Guide*

"Nationally known IRA expert James Lange provides the inside scoop on the strategies for how best to plan for IRAs under the new SECURE Act."

> — **Bruce D. Steiner, Esq.,**
> **Kleinberg, Kaplan, Wolff & Cohen, P.C.**

"Jim points out that under the new laws, your IRA is going to get crushed by taxation after your death and you have to do something about it. He lays out a number of excellent strategic options including charitable remainder trusts, Roth IRA conversions, and lifetime gifting. Every American with a significant IRA or retirement plan should read this book and consider implementing some, or all, of the strategic defenses Jim suggests."

> — **Larry Swedroe**, Chief Research Officer,
> **Buckingham Wealth Partners,**
> Author, *Your Complete Guide to a Successful & Secure Retirement*

"*Retire Secure!* is a very practical investment guide on how to defer taxes and efficiently plan for retirement and your estate."

— **Roger G. Ibbotson,** Professor, **Yale School of Management** and Chairman, **Ibbotson Associates**

"James Lange is a genius at making the most difficult subject of estate/retirement planning easy to understand. His book is an absolute must for anyone who wants the peace of mind that comes from knowing they will retire secure."

— **Eleanor Schano,** Former TV News Anchor, Host of **LifeQuest** (WQED Multimedia)

"*Retire Secure!* is the most well-written explanation of why maximizing the use of your retirement accounts, both tax-deferred and tax-free, will help you to retire with as much financial security as possible. Every serious individual investor should read this book!"

— **James M. Dahle, MD,** Author, *The White Coat Investor: A Doctor's Guide to Personal Finance and Investing*

"It is tough to pick stock-market winners, but it's relatively easy to lower your investment tax-bill. Looking to keep more of your portfolio's gains? Read Jim Lange's *The Roth Revolution*—and you could make your financial life a whole lot less taxing."

— **Jonathan Clements,** Author, *The Little Book of Main Street Money*

"Jim Lange hits another homerun with *The Roth Revolution*. Anyone concerned about ensuring his or her nest egg is enough for retirement needs this book... and that's just about all of us."

— **Lois P. Frankel, Ph.D.,** Author, *Nice Girls Don't Get Rich and Nice Girls Don't Get the Corner Office*

"*The Roth Revolution* is a clear and comprehensive guide to a financial planning tool everyone should understand. I highly recommend it."

— **Michael T. Palmero, Attorney at Law,** Author, *AARP Crash Course in Estate Planning*

"*The Roth Revolution* is must reading for anyone contemplating moving money into a Roth IRA, which in my opinion is everyone. Jim Lange is one of the few people who has the knowledge when it comes to IRAs and also has the ability to put this knowledge into understandable language."

— **Barry C. Picker, CPA/PFS, CFP, Picker & Auerbach, CPAs, P.C.**

"An amazing, comprehensive explanation of the hows and whys of Roth IRAs with real life examples unlocked by Jim Lange who has set a new standard in retirement tax planning."

— **Diane McCurdy, CFP,** Best-Selling Author,
*How Much is Enough? Balancing Today's Needs with
Tomorrow's Retirement Goals*

"Jim Lange has done it again! *The Roth Revolution* is a worthy follow up to *Retire Secure!*, written in a highly readable style that provides an excellent guide for all of us whose clients want to know whether they should convert to a Roth IRA. We were particularly pleased to find a thoughtful discussion of combining Roth IRAs with philanthropy."

— **Jon Gallo, J.D.,** Author, *The Financially Intelligent Parent:
8 Steps To Raising Successful, Generous, Responsible Children*

"Jim's specific advice to taxpayers in different tax brackets (Chapter Thirteen) in *The Roth Revolution* makes a complicated topic easy to understand."

— **Bill Losey, CFP,** Author, *Retire in a Weekend!
The Baby Boomer's Guide to Making Work Optional*

"This book shows you how to plan your finances so you don't run out of money in retirement—perhaps the biggest single consideration of your life."

— **Brian Tracy,** Author, *The Way to Wealth*

"Read James Lange's excellent book, *The $214,000 Mistake, How to Double Your Social Security & Maximize Your IRAs* and learn how and when to take your Social Security and retirement accounts. Doing so will pay for itself hundreds, if not thousands of times over."

— **Laurence Kotlikoff,** Author, *Get What's Yours*

"*The $214,000 Mistake, How to Double Your Social Security and Maximize Your IRAs* is the real deal. It delivers crucial, timely information about the new Social Security rules with clarity and precision and should be required reading for everyone age 62 to 70 who is, or ever was married."

— **Elaine Floyd, CFP,** Author,
Savvy Social Security Planning for Boomers

"Jim Lange's new book, *Live Gay, Retire Rich*, offers practical, easy to understand advice that same-sex couples can use to guide them as they begin a new and exciting chapter of their lives together."

— **Martin Sheen,** Actor, *The West Wing,* 1999–2006

"This is an exciting time to be part of the LGBTQ community in America and it also is an important moment to take advantage of the financial opportunities available to us. Jim Lange's book, *Live Gay, Retire Rich*, is an easy-to-understand and valuable tool that will help us navigate the financial waters and successfully plan for our future."

— **Billie Jean King,** Winner of 39 Grand Slam Tennis Titles
and Founder, **Billie Jean King Leadership Initiative**

"Think of *Retire Secure!* as a GPS for your money. You may know where you are and where you want to go, but you don't know how to get there. Jim offers the best routes." *(From the Foreword)*

— **Larry King,** *Larry King Now*

Acknowledgements

Though I am listed as the author, the truth is that this book is the product of a monumental team effort. I and the readers who find value in these pages are indebted to a team of the best CPAs, estate attorneys and other professionals I could possibly hope to work with.

Shirl Trefelner, CPA, CSRP, made major contributions to the "number crunching" effort by preparing the graphs and charts in the chapters as well as providing a technical review. She got to the point where she was afraid to talk to me fearing I would want another chart or an edit to an existing one! She showed a lot of patience working on the book while juggling her other responsibilities.

Matt Schwartz, Esq. worked through some of the fine legal points of the law with me and reviewed the book for technical accuracy. He has also been juggling multiple responsibilities but found time to add to and improve the book.

Steve Kohman, CPA, CSRP, CSEP and our veteran number-cruncher, made multiple contributions in the Roth IRA conversion section as well as the charitable remainder trust section.

Glenn Venturino, CPA, contributed to the tax-loss harvesting section.

Diane Markel, BASW, CPA, MBA and one of our long-time CPAs reviewed this book for technical accuracy.

Karen Mathias, Esq., our in-house Social Security expert, has provided excellent analysis on ways to optimize Social Security and on the advantages of combining Social Security strategies with Roth IRA conversions.

John Montoya, Esq. helped by researching the section on disabled beneficiaries.

Adam Romanoski, CPA also reviewed the book for technical accuracy.

Cynthia Nelson, our regular editor for twenty-three years, is not only a great editor, but her edits don't drown my voice, so my unique personality (and humor, where appropriate) is left intact after her edits. Humor is sorely needed because while I try to make it as entertaining as possible, it is still basically a book on cutting your taxes and could be a bit dry.

To that end, special thanks go to **Randy Bish** for the cartoons throughout the book and to **Carol Palmer** who had the inspiration for many of the cartoons. Carol was also extremely helpful in an earlier edition of this book before the law actually passed.

Sandy Proto both contributed to the editing and was hugely responsible for doing much of the behind the scenes work to make the book a success.

Erika Hubbard helped with the copy and beginning and ending sections of the book.

Bryan Tann lead the social media coverage of the book.

Eric Emerson led the marketing team efforts of the book.

Susan Abrams of **Abrams Design**, my graphic designer, designed the book and its cover, and added tone to the cartoons.

Other team members, though not directly involved with the book, allowed me and other team members the luxury of working on the book, and frankly we would not have a company without them. Special thanks to **Alice Davis, Donna Master, Daryl Ross, Sue Jeffries, Justin Pape** and **Jennifer Pickels** for all your contributions.

Finally, though many of the team members mentioned above have been with me for almost twenty years, special recognition to Glenn Venturino, Sandy Proto and Steve Kohman who have been with me close to thirty years.

To matters of the heart, a special thanks to my wife, **Cindy**, and my daughter, **Erica**. Cindy is probably the only woman alive who could put up with being married to me. This book would never have happened without Cindy's and Erica's love and support.

Thank you all.

Table of Contents

The IRA and Retirement Plan Owner's Guide to
Beating the New Death Tax:
6 Proven Strategies to Protect Your Family from The SECURE Act

by James Lange, CPA/Attorney

Overview

*"...The difference between death and taxes is
death doesn't get worse every time Congress meets."*

— **Will Rogers**

The overview provides a compressed, but packed, summary of the new law, and importantly, some of our favorite strategies for beating the new death tax. We strongly encourage you to read the entire overview. Once you have the big picture, you can scan the detailed Table of Contents for areas of particular interest to you. All of the information in this overview will be covered in greater detail in the chapters that follow.

Why the SECURE Act is So Devastating to IRA and Retirement Plan Owners

The ticking time bomb in the SECURE Act is the provision that radically modifies the required minimum distribution (RMD) rules for Inherited IRAs and retirement accounts. Subject to some exceptions, an Inherited IRA or retirement plan will have to be distributed and taxed within 10 years of the original owner's death[1], effectively cementing "the death of the stretch IRA."

---

[1] Technically, the account must all be withdrawn by December 31, of the 10th year after the death of the IRA owner. For example, if the IRA owner died on 1/1/2020, the heirs would have until 12/31/2030 to take all the money out of the account—effectively adding up to another year to the distribution period. This technical description will apply to all future references to the 10-year rule in this book.

Prior to the SECURE Act's passage, a non-spouse beneficiary of an Inherited IRA was permitted to minimize their tax burden by limiting distributions from the Inherited IRA to, depending on their age, a relatively small required minimum. The RMD of the Inherited IRA used to be calculated by dividing the balance in the Inherited IRA as of December 31st of the previous year by the life expectancy of the beneficiary. This, in effect, "stretched" distributions over the course of a lifetime. The lifetime "stretch" of the Inherited IRA allowed the beneficiary to keep the bulk of the Inherited IRA in a tax-deferred environment (for traditional IRAs) or a tax-free environment (for Roth IRAs).

The ticking time bomb in the SECURE Act is the provision that radically modifies the required minimum distribution (RMD) rules for Inherited IRAs and retirement accounts.

Bill, a well-loved client, died on December 29, 2019. Bill was a widower with one son, Bill Jr., who was the beneficiary of Bill's million-dollar IRA[2]. Bill Jr., like his dad, is a tax-savvy man. I have to confess that I, Matt Schwartz, our lead estate attorney, and Bill Jr., while of course saddened by Bill's death, took a bit of con-

---

[2] Please note that here and throughout the book, I mention situations and events as if the details are a literal portrayal of my firsthand experiences with clients. Actually, the opposite is true. I deliberately change names, sexes of the characters, facts, numbers, etc. from the actual circumstances. These anecdotes are generally inspired by real life situations, but any similarity to actual clients would be a total violation of confidentiality which is more important than accurately representing the facts of their situation. I do, however, use these anecdotes to demonstrate scenarios that are both plausible and based on real situations.

solation from the tax advantages that stemmed from Bill dying before year-end instead of several days later.

Bill Jr. was curious to understand what it would have meant to him financially if his father had died after January 1, 2020, the effective date of the SECURE Act instead of when he did.

We analyzed the difference. It was a good task, and one that we believe is instructive. It quantifies the financial difference for a beneficiary who inherited an IRA prior to and after the SECURE Act.

Here is a graph that demonstrates the difference to Bill Jr. of inheriting a million-dollar Traditional IRA under the prior law, and the current law under the SECURE Act.

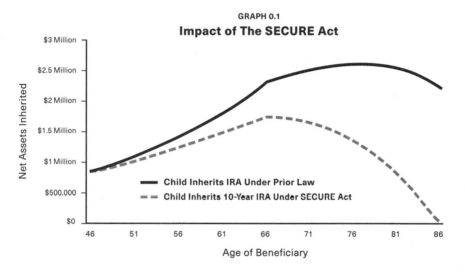

GRAPH 0.1
Impact of The SECURE Act

The only difference between those two scenarios is when the beneficiary pays taxes. The solid line represents the beneficiary who was able to stretch taxes over his lifetime under the old rules. Under the old law, using reasonable assumptions, the beneficiary of the inherited IRA would still have $2,236,583 when he is 86 years old. In sharp contrast, using identical assumptions, under the SECURE Act, the beneficiary would have $0. This is the difference between your child being financially secure versus being broke. Congress is trying to gloss over this point. "Secure?" I don't think so.

Eliminating the lifetime stretch robs IRA beneficiaries of decades upon decades of tax-deferred or tax-free growth. Even more importantly, it subjects the beneficiaries of traditional (tax-deferred) retirement plans to massive income-

---

> **Under the old law, using reasonable assumptions, the beneficiary
> of the inherited IRA would still have $2,236,583 when he is 86
> years old. In sharp contrast, using identical assumptions, under
> the SECURE Act, the beneficiary would have $0.**

---

tax acceleration. This will be especially brutal if the beneficiaries of the inherited IRA are working and have income of their own. If so, the added income from the accelerated withdrawals from the Inherited IRA could be taxed at even higher rates.

The change in these rules will result in a windfall to the IRS of billions of dollars at your children's expense.

There is a second point to consider with respect to income taxes. Beneficiaries of Inherited Traditional IRAs must pay tax on the withdrawal itself, but beneficiaries of Inherited Roth IRA accounts will not have to pay taxes on their withdrawals. Then, after either the Inherited Traditional IRA or Inherited Roth IRA is distributed within the 10 years after the death of the IRA owner, the earnings on the future withdrawals also lose the protection from income taxes. This is true whether the inherited account is a Traditional IRA or a Roth IRA. So if you are contemplating your estate plan, it is important to understand that your beneficiaries will have to pay taxes on the dividends, interest, and realized capital gains that are earned on the money they withdraw after the Inherited Traditional IRA or Inherited Roth IRA is distributed.

And the sooner the money is withdrawn from an Inherited IRA or Roth IRA, the sooner future interest, dividends and capital gains will be taxable.

Exceptions to the SECURE Act

The most important exception to the SECURE Act is that the law does not apply to IRAs that you leave to your surviving spouse. Your surviving spouse can still make a trustee-to-trustee transfer or a rollover of your IRA to her IRA—there is no change from the old law.

One surprising exception to the SECURE Act 10-year provision applies to non-spousal heirs who are not more than 10 years younger than the original IRA owner. This exception would most likely apply if you were to leave an IRA to a sibling or an unmarried partner. If you leave an IRA to your brother (who is

The most important exception to the SECURE Act is that the law does not apply to IRAs that you leave to your surviving spouse.

not more than 10 years younger than you), your brother will be able to stretch or defer taxable distributions of the Inherited IRA over his lifetime.

The SECURE Act includes an exception for children *while they are still considered minors* according to the law of the state in which they live. They also receive more favorable treatment. Once the minor children reach their majority, however, the 10-year clock starts ticking. The age of majority in Pennsylvania is 18. At this time, it is unclear, but the exception may also extend to children enrolled in school and under age 26.

Disabled and chronically ill beneficiaries are also exempt from the onerous distribution provisions of the SECURE Act. (Please read the extended footnote in Chapter 4 on page 53 for a description of who qualifies for the designation of disabled or chronically ill. Fair warning, if you don't like Congress now, your hatred will grow when you read the stringent requirements to be considered disabled.)

Finally, a critically important exception that IRA owners should know about is that charitable trusts will not be subject to the ten-year income tax acceleration of the SECURE Act. We have done the math and charitable trust planning could become one of the great defenses to the SECURE Act and should be strongly considered by many IRA owners, even if you aren't charitably inclined.

Some of the Goodies in the SECURE Act

The SECURE Act has been promoted as an "enhancement" for IRA and retirement plan owners because it includes some "Gift Horse" provisions that, subject to exception, are relatively insignificant for IRA and retirement plan owners who are retired or close to retirement.

The SECURE Act offers expanded opportunities for small employers to join "open multiple employer plans." This could be good for participants of small business retirement plans because it may increase investment options and reduce costs. In addition, part-time workers who were previously excluded are now permitted to participate in their employer's 401(k) plans.

The SECURE Act will increase opportunities for more lifetime-income op-

We have done the math and charitable trust planning could become one of the great defenses to the SECURE Act and should be strongly considered by many IRA owners, even if you aren't charitably inclined.

tions in employer's retirement plans—a provision that was pushed for by insurance companies that offer annuities. Frankly, this provision could dramatically increase the sale of high-cost, high-fee annuities inside retirement plans. I don't consider this a good thing for retirement plan participants. I would prefer if more retirement plan participants were offered retirement plan investment options that included low-cost well diversified index funds like many of the Vanguard funds.

The One Truly Worthwhile Provision of the SECURE Act

One provision in the SECURE Act that is genuinely useful and potentially significant is advancing the required minimum distribution (RMD) age to 72 instead of age 70½. The deadline for taking an RMD is April 1st of the year following the year you turn age 72—the law simply replaces age 70½ with age 72. But, as with the prior law, if you wait until April 1st of the year following the year you turn age 72, you have to take two distributions that year—one for the past year when you turned age 72, and one for the year you begin RMDs.

For many IRA owners, one of the best defenses against the death of the stretch IRA will be to complete a series of Roth IRA conversions, preferably during the years after they stop working but before they are required to take RMDs from their retirement plans. Once they are required to take taxable distributions from their traditional IRAs, IRA owners may find themselves in a higher tax bracket. Additional income will also likely come from Social Security benefits. There is no good reason to hold off taking Social Security after you reach age 70. After the higher income from Social Security and your RMD kicks in, it may

One provision in the SECURE Act that is genuinely useful and potentially significant is advancing the required minimum distribution (RMD) age to 72 instead of age 70½.

not be favorable—or as favorable—to execute either a single year or a series of Roth IRA conversions. The change in the RMD rules will give many IRA owners two additional years of lower income to proactively make Roth IRA conversions before their RMD kicks in.

Please note that one of the favorable provisions of the CARES Act is that there is no RMD for 2020 which makes Roth IRA conversions that much more favorable. Please see Chapter 6.

More Opportunities for IRA and Back-Door Roth IRA Contributions

Another bit of good news for workers in their 70s and beyond is that the SECURE Act also eliminates the age 70½ cutoff for making traditional IRA contributions and allows workers of any age to continue adding to their retirement savings. This will make it possible for working seniors to make IRA contributions and even more "back-door" Roth IRA contributions, currently blessed by the Tax Cuts and Jobs Act.

We love "back-door" Roth IRA contributions. A back-door Roth IRA allows you to get around the income limitation on contributions to a Roth IRA. The IRS established income limits for taxpayers who want to contribute to Roth IRAs, which prevents higher-income individuals from saving in a tax-free environment. For 2020 you can't make a Roth IRA contribution if you are married and your modified adjusted gross income is more than $196,000 or more than $124,000 if you are single. But you might be able to get around those limitations with a back-door Roth IRA conversion.

The back-door Roth IRA is a technique where you set up and make contributions to a Traditional IRA because your income is too high for you to contribute directly to a Roth IRA. Then, assuming you don't have an existing Traditional IRA, you immediately convert the contribution you made to the Traditional IRA to a Roth IRA. This technique, something I have been doing and advocating for years, will now be available to working seniors. (There was never an age limitation on Roth IRA conversions, just traditional IRA contributions). As an aside, you can make a back-door Roth IRA contribution for your spouse, even if he or she is not working. I have been making back-door Roth IRA contributions for years and my wife, Cindy, who doesn't work outside the home also makes a back-door Roth IRA contribution.

To be more specific, Cindy and I are married, our modified adjusted gross income exceeds $196,000, we are both 50 or older and neither of us has a Traditional IRA. We made two $7,000 back-door Roth IRA contributions at the beginning of 2020 for tax year 2020. (The maximum Roth IRA contribution allowed is $6,000 per person and an extra $1,000 catch up for taxpayers 50 and older.) The contribution is due by April 15th after year-end, but you can contribute before year-end and if you contribute earlier in the year, you get an extra year of tax-free growth. Please note that the deadline for 2020 under the CARES Act is July 15th instead of April 15th.

The SECURE Act is Bad for Retirees

These minor positive provisions of the SECURE Act have negligible positive impact compared to the damage it is doing to older IRA and retirement plan owners. The SECURE Act is a travesty. It puts hard working IRA and retirement plan owners at an extreme disadvantage. The deal all along was that if you put money in an IRA or retirement plan, your kids would get favorable tax treatment after you die. Now, late in the game, the government is effectively saying "We changed our minds and we are changing the rules." It's bad news, and a betrayal of those Americans who saved for years in their retirement plans. The government made a set of laws and we relied on those laws, making major sacrifices to contribute to our IRAs and retirement plans. The legal term for this is "detrimental reliance." Unfortunately, in this case, we can't sue the government. All we can do is to radically change our planning in a way to best protect our families. I am fired up to help IRA and retirement plan owners reduce the impact of this draconian law.

Beating the New Death Tax

Though every taxpayer's financial situation is unique, there are certain strategies that will help many IRA and retirement plan owners beat the new death tax. One of the common themes of these recommendations is "die with a reduced balance in your traditional IRA or retirement plan so it will not be clobbered with taxes so quickly after you die."

Roth IRA Conversions

I have written and spoken extensively about the benefits of Roth IRA conversions in the past. Before, my thinking was that Roth IRA conversions not only had benefits for the IRA owner, but also allowed many years of tax-free growth for their children and even grandchildren. So, it was really more of an offensive strategy to get more tax-free income to three generations.

Now, the Roth IRA conversion, while still favorable under the SECURE Act,

---

Now, late in the game, the government is effectively saying "We changed our minds and we are changing the rules."

---

is really a defensive strategy that stops the IRS from having a huge payday at your death. As we go to press, the S&P has dropped roughly 10% from its peak due to COVID-19. Roth IRA conversions become that much more attractive if you think the market will eventually rebound.

Let's say you have a Traditional IRA that is invested in a low-cost index fund that was valued at $133,000 at its peak and today its value is $100,000. You can make a Roth IRA conversion on the $100,000 now and pay tax (using money from outside of your IRA) on $100,000. The market rebounds to its pre-crash level and now your Roth IRA is worth $133,000. You just got a great bargain by paying tax on $100,000 and getting a $133,000 tax-free Roth IRA in return.

The $2 trillion dollar Coronavirus Aid, Relief, and Economic Security Act (CARES Act) temporarily suspends the RMD requirement from Traditional IRAs and retirement plans. If you are currently taking RMDs from your IRAs, consider foregoing that distribution in 2020 unless you need the money and depend on it for your cash flow. With respect to Roth IRA conversions, not taking a distribution from a Traditional IRA can make doing a Roth IRA conversion even more desirable because it might keep or put you in a favorable tax bracket by reducing your taxable income. If you were already planning on a Roth IRA conversion perhaps this will give you an opportunity to convert an even larger amount.

For most taxpayers, a properly timed series of Roth IRA conversions can be an effective strategic planning tool and a very good response to the death of the stretch IRA.

One good thing about the Tax Cuts and Jobs Act of 2017 (this is not a misprint) is that it temporarily lowered income tax rates, so that 2020 and beyond (until taxes are raised again), are probably better than average years for many IRA and retirement plan owners to make Roth IRA conversions—assuming it is a good plan in the first place. If you think income tax rates are going to go up in the future, which is even more likely because someone will have to pay for the CARES Act, Roth IRA conversions become an even more promising method of cutting taxes for you and your family. The combination of the market and income taxes being down, and the suspension of the RMD make now perhaps the best time in history for many IRA owners to make a Roth IRA conversion of a portion of their IRA. We go into much greater detail on the impact of the changing tax rates for Roth IRA conversions in Chapter 6.

Many advisors are telling their clients to rebalance now, meaning buy more stocks when the market is low. Given everything else that is going on with the disruption of COVID-19, that advice, though probably good in the long run, is not comfortable. What if the market stays flat for a long time? But, with a Roth IRA conversion, even if the market stays flat, you and your family will likely be better off. In addition, if the market does go back up, the tax savings will be enormous.

Often, a reasonable starting point for developing a long-term Roth IRA conversion plan strategy is to make a series of Roth IRA conversions over a period of years so the conversions don't push you into a higher tax-bracket for income tax purposes, Social Security taxability purposes and Medicare Part B purposes. But that is a starting point, not an ending point.

Roth IRA conversions are extremely valuable. However, determining the right amount to convert, when to convert, and whether you should convert a certain amount over a number of years usually requires careful consideration. The assistance of a qualified advisor who understands both numbers and the tax code, most likely a CPA, is strongly recommended. Converting even a portion of your IRA could provide an enormous benefit to you and your family—but individual circumstances must be evaluated.

One negative recent change to the Roth IRA conversion law is that you are no longer allowed to make a Roth IRA conversion and undo it (technically recharacterize the Roth IRA conversion). Under old law, you could make a Roth IRA conversion and if the underlying investment went down or you changed your mind, you could undo it or technically recharacterize the Roth IRA conversion. No longer.

That said, usually the tough part is deciding how much and when you should convert to a Roth IRA. If you have a CPA or an advisor who has expertise in Roth IRA conversions, consult them. If you don't have an appropriate advisor and would like some help in this area, please see our offer on page 175 at the end of the book.

Social Security Planning

If you have not already applied for Social Security (or even if you have and are younger than 70 years old), you may benefit from reconsidering your Social Security strategy. If you haven't applied, consider waiting until age 70 to do so.

The monetary value of postponing future benefits from age 66 to 70 will be to increase your benefit by 8% per year, and potentially for your surviving spouse, for the rest of your lives. If you are at least full retirement age which varies depending on the year you were born, (but if you were born between 1943 and 1954, it is age 66) and have been receiving Social Security benefits, you can often choose to temporarily stop receiving benefits—that is, to postpone them until you turn 70. This will increase the value of your future benefits by 8% for every year you wait.

The reason that a well-planned Social Security strategy can help you beat the new death tax is that, by holding off or stopping your Social Security checks, you will likely be able to reduce your taxable income. This may allow you to make bigger Roth IRA conversions, potentially at lower tax rates.

Combining Roth IRA Conversions and Social Security Strategies Can be Advantageous for You Even Without Considering Your Heirs

We have talked a lot about the value of Roth IRA conversions for your heirs. But the appropriate series of Roth IRA conversions will likely substantially improve not only your financial legacy, but also your financial position. And when you combine the Social Security strategy and Roth conversions, you can maximize the benefits to you and your spouse (see Chapter 14).

I was meeting with a married couple, Joe and Michelle, who attended my workshop and hoped I was wrong about Social Security. They had been following the advice that Joe received from a well-known and highly respected advisor. His advisor advocated taking Social Security at age 62 as long as you were retired, and discouraged Joe and Michelle from making any Roth IRA conversions. Their old advisor told Joe and Michelle that they had worked hard all their lives and they should enjoy their retirement years without having to economize. I agreed. That was one of the few areas in which I agreed with their old advisor.

I wanted Joe to hold off on Social Security until he was age 70 and make a series of Roth IRA conversions.

What Joe didn't get was that our recommendations would give him and Michelle a lot more disposable income and dramatically reduce the chances they would run out of money. These benefits were over and above the benefit of leaving a lot more money for their children.

At the risk of sounding arrogant, I don't believe the disagreement I have with Joe's former advisor on the issue of holding off on Social Security and making a series of Roth IRA conversions is simply a difference of opinion that can never be resolved with clarity one way or the other. Let me offer an analogy. For many readers, Celine Dion is their favorite female singer. Personally, I prefer Whitney Houston, though I love them both. Holding a personal preference is totally legitimate in that situation. But not with Social Security and Roth IRA conversions because...

You can "run the numbers." You can make reasonable assumptions and make projections. You can see where you will be if you collect Social Security early and don't make Roth IRA conversions and contrast that with holding off until age 70 to take Social Security and making a series of Roth IRA conversions. You can also run the numbers using your children's life expectancy as an endpoint.

Yes, you can disagree on the assumptions, but I resolve that issue in practice by running the numbers with assumptions I think are reasonable, or preferably, we run the numbers with the client's input on reasonable assumptions.

Joe was stubborn and truly hoped I was wrong. He didn't like starting a strategy (in this case taking Social Security early and not doing Roth IRA conversions) and then switching midway through. The good thing, however, was that Joe was data driven, and if you could prove it to Joe on a spreadsheet that he could closely examine, he was capable of changing his mind.

Anyway, we ran the numbers for Joe and Michelle. Again, you can challenge

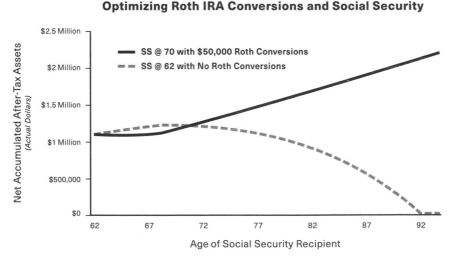

GRAPH 0.2
Optimizing Roth IRA Conversions and Social Security

Please see detailed assumptions in the Appendix.

the assumptions, but the math is the math and not a matter of opinion. We believe you can get dramatically better results by "running the numbers" and comparing different strategies than if you just guess. We ran the numbers and arrived at the conclusion I expected—hold off on Social Security and make a series of Roth IRA conversions. Please see the chart at the bottom of page 12 that demonstrates the results of "running the numbers" for Joe and Michelle, not even taking into consideration the benefits to their children.

To be more specific, the chart shows a difference of over $2,000,000 between Joe and Michelle optimizing Roth IRA conversions and Social Security strategies versus collecting Social Security early and not doing any Roth IRA conversions. Before we ran the numbers, Joe thought the Roth IRA conversions would be great for his kids, but not for him and Michelle.

At first, Joe didn't accept this conclusion. Joe thought my Roth IRA conversion recommendation was based on what was better for his kids over the long run. When he looked at the spreadsheets and had the opportunity to challenge our assumptions and calculations, we were eventually able to satisfy him. He began to think differently about his financial strategy. That is the advantage of having the skeptical IRA owner in the room (or via remote conferencing, which is how we have been having meetings lately, when we "run the numbers"). The good news was that even though Joe was a little bit head-strong (Michelle laughed when I said that), he was data driven.

Putting these strategies in place would allow both Joe and Michelle to significantly reduce their chances of outliving their money and significantly *increase* the amount of money they could safely spend. For them, it made a dramatic difference.

If you dig deeply into the numbers, the details of which we do not include in this book, the change in Social Security strategy amounted to less than $200,000.

What is so exciting about this graph is that it shows that two of the major strategies we use to defend your legacy from the SECURE Act provide an enormous benefit for you and your spouse. Specifically: holding off on Social Security and making a series of Roth IRA conversions, helps you and your spouse and your family.

It was the series of Roth IRA conversions that made the significant difference. If you want to take it a step deeper, holding off on Social Security lowered Joe's income which allowed greater Roth IRA conversions at lower tax rates.

What this shows is that optimizing Roth IRA conversions and Social Security is really a synergistic calculation. Simply doing Roth conversions without holding off on Social Security would have diminished the benefit of the Roth conversions compared to the benefit of Roth conversions while holding off on Social Security.

What is so exciting about this graph is that it shows that two of the major strategies we use to defend your legacy from the SECURE Act provide an enormous benefit for you and your spouse. Specifically: holding off on Social Security and making a series of Roth IRA conversions, helps you and your spouse and your family. You could look at the enormous savings for your children and grandchildren as a bonus. But the bottom line is that it is likely great for you.

Incidentally, the benefits of holding off on Social Security and doing a series of Roth conversions, for many, if not most IRA owners, was true both before and after the SECURE Act.

Review Your Estate Plan Including Wills, Trusts, and the Beneficiary Designations of your Retirement Plan

Thoughtful estate planning is critical. Reviewing and possibly updating your entire estate plan, including wills, trusts, and IRA beneficiary designations is a good idea for many IRA and retirement plan owners. This is particularly true if you have established trusts for any beneficiary or even a contingent beneficiary of your IRA or retirement plan. The use of disclaimers appropriately offers flexibility to many estate plans. If you have any type of conduit trust in your existing estate planning documents, it may now do more harm than good. You should contact your attorney if your estate plan needs to be updated, because beating the new death tax could very well mean hundreds of thousands of dollars to your heirs. We discuss both disclaimers and conduit trusts in greater detail in Chapter 2.

In my humble opinion, if your estate plan needs to be updated as a result of the SECURE Act, the estate attorney who drafted your last set of wills, trusts and IRA beneficiary designations *should be contacting you.* That is what our law office started to do with our clients who need to update their documents. To be fair, the COVID-19 disruption has created other priorities and as we go to press, we are way behind contacting all the clients we want to contact.

In fairness to your estate attorney—who likely will not contact you or at most will send a general notification—few law firms are pro-active enough to alert clients that their documents should be updated as a consequence of a new law. We get a lot of new legal business not necessarily because the client was unhappy with the previous estate attorney who did their estate plan, but rather because that attorney never communicated with the client after the documents were signed and notarized.

If our law firm did your estate plan and drafted your wills, trusts, IRA beneficiary designations, etc.—even 20 years ago—and you did nothing else with us, you would have received books, articles, monthly hard-copy newsletters, countless invitations to workshops, tax cards, etc. Just last year you would have received 12 hard-copy newsletters, a series of articles, a tax card, gobs of emails, an earlier version of this book predicting the "death of the stretch IRA" that made recommendations about what to do about it and much more. Then, depending on whether we think your documents need to be updated, we will personally reach out to you this year. It is a massive job because we have completed 2,769 estate plans including wills and trusts, etc. It is a little bit like triage in that we are contacting our clients who most desperately need to change their documents. We are even more pro-active with our assets-under-management clients.

We think communicating with all our clients frequently is good business.

Gifting to Children and Grandchildren

Many families should now consider making significant gifts to their children and grandchildren. The source of the funds for the gifts could come from distributions from your IRA, even reduced by the income taxes on the withdrawal. Then, with the money that you have after paying taxes, you could make a gift to your family. This is another form of reducing the balance of your traditional IRA and beating the new death tax. You likely feel much poorer and fearful after the market impact of COVID-19. I know my wife Cindy has been cutting her spending, even though I haven't been cutting mine. So, I recognize a lot of it isn't math, it is mindset. That might be sufficient reason to reduce gifting or possibly stop making gifts, but don't take gifting strategies off the table unless you are pretty sure you cannot afford the gifts.

Of course, gifting can take on many flavors. It could be a straight-forward gift. "Here is some money." It could be a contribution to a 529 plan (tax-free college funding mechanism). It could provide money that your beneficiaries might use to contribute to their own Roth IRAs or Roth 401(k)s. It could even pay for premiums on a life insurance policy, the proceeds of which are tax-free and, assuming it is handled correctly, inheritance and estate tax-free.

Taking a taxed distribution from a Traditional IRA and offering the money to fund a 529 plan or life insurance or even a child's personal Roth IRA contribution is conceptually similar to a Roth IRA conversion. Effectively, you pay tax up front in return for tax-free income. One difference between doing a Roth IRA conversion and withdrawing from an IRA so that you can make a gift to your children is that assets such as a 529 plan, life insurance (again, assuming that it is set up correctly) and your children's Roth IRAs is that these gifts will not be a part of your estate whereas the Roth IRA will be part of your estate.

Spending More Money

Most of my clients and readers don't spend as much money as they can afford to spend. When the tax ramifications of the SECURE Act sink in and they realize how their IRAs and retirement plans will be taxed unfairly after they die, maybe they will be more open to spending money now. (But probably not.) This is particularly true after COVID-19. But even if your portfolio is down quite a bit, does that mean you should deprive yourself of certain pleasures that cost money?

One of my favorite topics to discuss with clients is the benefits of taking their families on an annual vacation. Perhaps now that isn't feasible, but hopefully it will be in the future. If you can afford it, I recommend you do it every year and treat your entire family. My family does. My 25-year-old daughter, an only child, feels like she is part of a clan because she spends four days annually with her cousins and her 95-year-old grandfather, who pays for these annual gatherings. Even now with physical get togethers out of the question, she is enjoying Zoom calls with her cousins. This bond would never have happened without Grandpa footing the bill for these vacations. On a smaller scale, I just hosted a small family reunion. The family memories that you leave behind will be a much more valuable legacy *than a slightly bigger IRA that will get clobbered with taxes after you die.*

Charitable Remainder Trusts Even If You Aren't Charitable

For the first time in history, naming a charitable remainder trust as the beneficiary of your IRA could be more favorable to your children than if you name your children directly as the beneficiary of your IRA.

Charitable trusts are one of the critical exceptions to the ten-year income acceleration after an IRA owner's death. We present analysis in Chapter 8 showing

One of my favorite topics to discuss with clients is the benefits of taking their families on an annual vacation.

that using reasonable assumptions, your children will be better off by $465,175 if you leave your million-dollar traditional IRA to a charitable remainder trust rather than leaving the IRA to your children outright. To put it another way, when you compare leaving your million-dollar IRA to your child or to a charitable remainder trust given the same assumptions, including spending, your child will have $465,175 when he is 81 if you set up a charitable remainder trust. He will be broke at age 81 if you leave your million-dollar IRA to him outright. Another winner with this strategy is the charity that gets $452,211. The big loser is the IRS.

Yes, I concede the charity will have to wait a long time before they receive funds from the trust, but the numbers are compelling. In addition, many IRA owners will prefer that their children get an income for their entire lives rather than inheriting a huge IRA, paying enormous taxes, and then investing what is left.

But, before getting immersed in the details, just think of the benefits of a strategy that allows more money to go to your children as well as providing a substantial amount of money to a worthy charity. I have never been as excited about the prospects of benefitting your children and charity. *My new goal is to help direct a billion dollars to charity. I urge you to read Chapter 8 thoroughly as it may be a great solution for your family.*

Chapter 9 analyzes the best dollars to leave to charity in your estate plan. To simplify, leave your IRA money to charity and your after-tax dollars and Roth IRAs to your family. The following point was true before the SECURE Act, but the benefits of getting this right are even more significant after the SECURE Act.

Let's assume you want to leave $100,000 to XYZ charity at your death. If you leave $100,000 to the charity in your will or revocable trust, which controls your non-IRA and nonretirement plan money (which I refer to as "after-tax dollars"), then it will cost your family $100,000. If you name the charity as the beneficiary of $100,000 of your IRA, the cost of the donation to your heirs might be only $65,000. This is because the charity is tax-exempt, but your heirs are not. Your heirs might owe up to 35 percent in income tax when they withdraw money from the Inherited IRA. By changing the source of your charitable dollars from your will or trust, to a designated charity as a partial beneficiary of your IRA, you

For the first time in history, naming a charitable remainder trust as the beneficiary of your IRA could be more favorable to your children than if you name your children directly as the beneficiary of your IRA.

can dramatically decrease the taxes on your family while still providing for your favorite charities.

Practically all of the wills and trusts we see prepared by other attorneys, including some of the better-known estate planning attorneys from big firms that should know better, miss this easy technique. Missing this strategy could cost your family tens if not hundreds of thousands of dollars. Please see Chapters 8 and 9 for more details.

In Chapter 10, we show that charitable gifting directly from a traditional IRA (called a Qualified Charitable Distribution, or QCD) can help reduce the balance in your IRA, and ultimately help your beneficiary beat the death tax on their inheritance. Another benefit of a QCD is that it reduces your current taxable income, potentially making a partial Roth IRA conversion more attractive. QCDs have only recently been enacted on a permanent basis and understanding them and using them could provide enormous benefits for your favorite charities while cutting your taxes. Unfortunately, they only apply to IRA owners who are age 70½ or older.

Sprinkle Trusts

Sprinkle trusts, when used optimally, might provide families with opportunities to reduce the impact of the new death tax by spreading the tax burden from Inherited IRAs among multiple generations, including children, grandchildren and great-grandchildren. They could also be used to protect beneficiaries

My new goal is to help direct a billion dollars to charity. I urge you to read Chapter 8 thoroughly as it may be a great solution for your family.

in vulnerable life situations by retaining the income for their benefit in the trust. Sprinkle trusts have been one of the many "tools" in the sophisticated estate planner's repertoire for years. Now, they are much more attractive because they could result in significant tax benefits. (See Chapter 11.)

Things the Beneficiary of Your IRA Should Know

The above points apply to individuals who own IRAs, but there are some things that IRA beneficiaries should be aware of too. If owners of Inherited IRAs are not proactive, the new death tax will cost them dearly.

The best time to take a taxable withdrawal from a Traditional Inherited IRA would be when your beneficiary is in their lowest tax bracket, as long as it is within 10 years of the death of the IRA owner. If the beneficiary inherits a Roth IRA, he or she should consider maintaining the tax-free growth in the account for 10 years after the death of the original owner.

In conclusion, *now is not the time for IRA and retirement plan owners to be complacent.* Congress is attacking your family's financial security and it is time to act.

Why are IRA Owners leaving their local planners and coming to a small Western PA office for advice?

Did your advisor give you actionable steps that will save you and your family a lot of money like you have already received after just reading the overview? Could the new SECURE Act and COVID-19 and CARES have wide-reaching financial consequences for you, your spouse, and even your children and grandchildren?

Most likely, yes. But how can the SECURE Act harm you financially? And more importantly, are there steps you can take to mitigate the damage...and even make the SECURE Act, COVID-19 and CARES work to your financial benefit?

Now, it can cost you *nothing* to find out...when you accept our offer of a FREE, no-obligation ***Retire Secure Initial Consultation***.

You'll get a confidential, informed, and accurate reading on how the SECURE Act, COVID-19 and CARES are going to affect your retirement and estate planning. And you'll discover what you can do now to map out a clear course of action for securing your family's financial future.

To protect your health as well as your wealth during the COVID-19 pandemic, Retire Secure Consultations are now being offered remotely via phone, or Zoom. That means YOU can stay home...and stay safe... and get an expert "second opinion" review of your financial ability to retire secure for life, when you meet with us "virtually."

Up until just recently we were planning to charge $997 for this consultation unless you came to Pittsburgh and had the consultation in person. Since that isn't a viable option, at least for now, we decided to open the free consultations to qualified IRA and retirement plan owners throughout the country.

There is no cost for your virtual *Retire Secure Initial Consultation*, either by phone or online. If you qualify, it's yours free of charge. For more information to see if you qualify and to schedule your free *Retire Secure Initial Consultation*, call us toll-free today at **1-800-387-1129** or go to **page 175**.

1

The Bedrock Principle of Retirement and Estate Planning

*"Anyone may arrange his affairs so that his taxes shall be
as low as possible; he is not bound to choose that pattern which
best pays the treasury. There is not even a patriotic duty to
increase one's taxes"*

— **Judge Learned Hand**

Pay Taxes Later—Except for Roths

Don't pay taxes now, pay taxes later, except for the Roth. These words represent the *bedrock* principle of tax planning for accumulating and distributing wealth. It is critical in the accumulation stage when you are saving for retirement. It is essential in the distribution stage when you are withdrawing money from your portfolio after you retire. And it can dramatically improve the financial lives of your heirs in the estate-planning stage.

The SECURE Act's radically modified required minimum distribution (RMD) rules for Inherited IRAs and retirement accounts force your heirs to pay taxes much sooner. That is a major problem.

For many of us, our IRAs and retirement plans hold the bulk of our wealth, so planning for the disposition of your IRA is critically important.

I did say "except for the Roth." But it is not possible to cover all the best strategies for Roths and Roth conversions in this mercifully short book. For more information comparing Roth IRAs, Roth 401(k)s and Roth 403(b)s to traditional retirement accounts and the related issues of Roth IRA conversions, please go to **https://paytaxeslater.com/books/** and download a free copy of our best-

Jim's Mantra, *Pay Taxes Later*, is Our Bedrock Principle

selling book, ***The Roth Revolution, Pay Taxes Once and Never Again.*** If you are interested in Roth IRAs and Roth IRA conversions, and you probably should be, at a minimum, please read Chapter 1 of that book. You can also get a hard copy or digital copy from Amazon. To some extent, however, we will cover Roth IRA conversions in this book because we use it as a strategy to protect your wealth from excessive taxes. It is one of our defenses to the devastation of the SECURE Act.

Saving for Retirement while Working

Make no bones about it: taking advantage of employer-matching contributions to any retirement plan is the cardinal rule of saving for your old age. For workers early in their career, a bear market is more advantageous than a bull market because there is an even greater potential for growth.

If an employer match is available to you, then make sure you are participating in your employer's retirement plan. It's like free money—and all the money in your retirement plan grows either tax-deferred, as is the case with a Traditional 401(k), or tax-free with a Roth 401(k). If your employer offers matching opportunities plus a Roth 401(k), you will have the option to make contributions to either the Traditional 401(k) or the Roth 401(k). The employer's contribution, however, will always be into the Traditional 401(k), not the Roth 401(k), though the employer could match your Roth 401(k) contribution with a Traditional 401(k) contribution.

After taking advantage of the employer's matching contribution, the next area you should consider, assuming your employer offers one, are contributions to your Health Savings Account (HSA). Your HSA is even better than a Roth. You get a tax deduction for your contribution, it grows tax-free and, assuming you withdraw it to pay for qualified medical expenses, the distribution is tax-free. We will not provide any further coverage regarding HSAs in this book, but since this section is on the best way to save for retirement, I would be remiss in not mentioning HSAs.

Then, after the matching contribution and the HSA, the next priority during the accumulation stage (subject to exceptions determined by personal circumstances) is to contribute to any available Roth IRAs, Roth 401(k)s, and Roth 403(b)s.

By the way, employers would be well advised to offer, at a minimum, a Roth 401(k) component to their existing retirement plan options. That will not cost them any money. They should also offer an HSA that will not cost them much. Both types of plans provide great benefits for their employees. We offer both of those benefits to our employees as well as traditional benefits like a good healthcare plan, dental, vision, disability, life insurance, etc. I am sure these benefits contribute to how little turnover of our top talent we have experienced in the last 20 years.

If your employer doesn't offer a Roth 401(k) or you don't qualify for a Roth IRA contribution because your income is too high and you can't do a back-door Roth IRA contribution, consider the next priority which would be to save inside a Traditional 401(k), 403(b) IRA or even an IRA. This is a topic that I write about at length in my flagship book, *Retire Secure! Third Edition.* You can get a digital copy of the best-selling book, *Retire Secure!*, for free by going to **https://paytax eslater.com/books/**. My flagship book can also be ordered in either the digital or hard copy format from Amazon.

There really isn't the space in this short book to address all the arguments or present the comprehensive analysis we did in *Retire Secure!* for saving in re-

---

Your HSA is even better than a Roth. You get a tax deduction for your contribution, it grows tax-free and, assuming you withdraw it to pay for qualified medical expenses, the distribution is tax-free.

tirement plans versus taxable accounts. But we have done the math and we also compare the Roth vs. Traditional even forgetting the employer match. So, for the sake of simplicity, I offer Graph 1.1 as proof of the value of saving in retirement accounts as opposed to a regular investment account (labeled after-tax funds). The graph that follows shows the difference in savings over a lifetime.

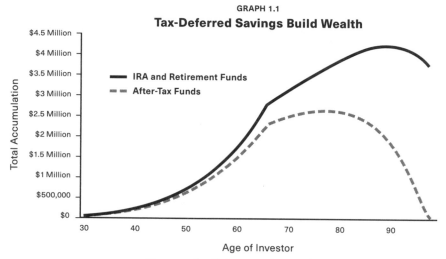

GRAPH 1.1
Tax-Deferred Savings Build Wealth

Please see detailed assumptions in the Appendix.

The individual who used his employer's retirement plan enjoyed immediate tax savings when making contributions and enjoyed tax-deferred growth during the investment years. You do, however, have to pay taxes when you begin taking distributions. The individual who saved outside of his employer's retirement plan didn't get a tax break up front, and had to pay taxes on the interest, dividends and realized capital gains every year. The employee who used his employer's plan had $1,118,724 more at age 80 than the employee who did not invest in his employer's plan, even though the amount of money they saved on a tax-adjusted basis was the same. This graph reflects our basic premise, that

---

The employee who used his employer's plan had $1,118,724 more at age 80 than the employee who did not invest in his employer's plan, even though the amount of money they saved on a tax-adjusted basis was the same.

---

paying taxes later while you are in the accumulation stage means you can retire richer instead of "broker."

We have also analyzed the issue of saving in Roth IRAs or Roth 401(k)s versus Traditional IRAs and 401(k)s. Though the difference is not nearly as dramatic, subject to exceptions, workers contributing to Roth IRAs and Roth 401(k)s will usually be much better off in the long run than workers contributing to Traditional IRAs and 401(k)s.

Please note that with the SECURE Act, there is an even greater incentive to contribute to Roth IRAs and Roth 401(k)s as opposed to Traditional IRAs and 401(k)s because the Roths will be an even more valuable asset to leave behind.

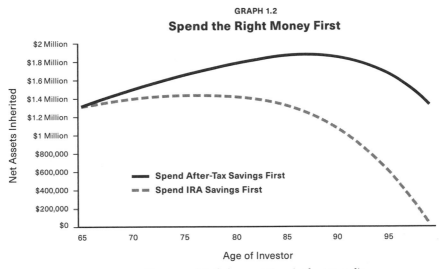

GRAPH 1.2
Spend the Right Money First

Please see detailed assumptions in the Appendix.

Spend the Right Money First when You Retire

The next big question is: In what order should you spend the money that you have saved for retirement? Subject to exception, and under the SECURE Act the exceptions are bigger than ever, please spend your after-tax dollars before your IRA or retirement plan dollars.

Look at the graph above. Both couples start with the same amount of money in a traditional brokerage account—which I refer to as after-tax dollars—and in their IRAs. The graph below indicates, subject to exceptions, that most readers should spend their after-tax dollars first and then IRAs and retirement plans dollars. The solid line shows what happens to the first couple who spend their after-tax dollars first and withdraw only the minimum from the IRA when they are required to (more on RMDs in the next section). This is the *pay-taxes-later* application. The dotted line shows what happens to the second couple who spend their IRA first. This is the *pay-taxes-now* application.

The only difference between the dotted line and the solid line in this graph is that the first couple retained more money in the tax-deferred IRA for a longer period. Even starting at age 65, the decision to defer income taxes for as long as possible gives the first couple an extra $625,591 if the couple live to age 87.

If one of them lives longer, paying taxes later will be even more valuable to them. In addition, subject to exception, in general the last dollars you want to spend are your Roth IRA dollars.

Subject to exception, you and your spouse will realize a benefit by deferring the income taxes due on your retirement plans for as long as possible. With the SECURE Act now part of the law, if you and your spouse continue this strategy and money remains in your IRAs and retirement accounts after your death, your children and grandchildren (subject to some exceptions) will have to pay income taxes on the Inherited IRA within 10 years of your death. This was, and frequently still is, the prudent order for many IRA owners to spend their money.

Under the SECURE Act, however, adhering to the pay-taxes-later rule in the distribution stage is a much tougher call and must be analyzed on a case by case basis. It might be better for your children if you spend your IRA or retirement plan first. For your children, losing the lifetime stretch on an inherited retirement account carries a huge tax burden. We will cover the impact of the new law in Chapter 3.

Of course, sometimes it makes sense to distribute IRAs before other funds to take advantage of a low-income tax bracket. When I run into that situation, I also think about Roth IRA conversions.

There is one important consequence of the Tax Cut and Jobs Act of 2017 (that isn't a misprint, I am talking about an older law that has a huge impact today) that I want to address as it relates to the SECURE Act. The 2017 Act included a temporary reduction of the income tax brackets. In 2017, the 25% tax bracket used to top out at $153,100 for a married couple. In 2020, the 24% tax bracket tops out at $326,600. These reduced tax rates are scheduled to revert to the old rates at the end of 2025. They also might go up with a change of administration. In addition, someone is going to have to pay for the bailouts the government provided both before and after the COVID-19 pandemic. Who will that someone be? Probably you and your family and others in a similar situation.

Still, you might be thinking, "What are you talking about, Jim? My income isn't anywhere near $326,600 now that I am retired." True, but even if your taxable income is $100,000, you can now either withdraw or make a Roth IRA conversion of up to $226,000 and still be in the 24% tax bracket. In 2017, that would have put you in the 33% bracket. So, before you say that taking distributions from your IRA above the minimum or, better yet, making a series of Roth IRA conversions aren't for me, please be open minded and examine the data. (In God We Trust, all others bring data.) If you think the market will follow history and eventually recover, Roth IRA conversions will be even more profitable for you and your family.

Annually, we "run the numbers" for our assets-under-management clients. "Running the numbers" is our shorthand term for preparing a detailed quantitative analysis of a client's finances and financial decisions. We test the tax implications of a variety of different scenarios based on varying assumptions. We were relatively sure that the SECURE Act or something like it was coming—including the likely acceleration of income taxes of Inherited IRAs as well as the likely income tax increases—and we included those assumptions in many of the different scenarios in our projections for the last five years.

We found ourselves recommending that many 70+ year old clients continue executing Roth conversions even though they were already taking RMDs and receiving Social Security benefits. Though every taxpayer has unique circumstances, it is an interesting idea to consider making Roth conversions in the 24% tax bracket when you know future RMDs will be taxed at an equal or higher tax rates once your RMD and the current tax rates increase. This strategy could be extremely valuable to you, as well as to your heirs down the road.

The point is that just because you are taking minimum distributions and Social Security, don't assume you aren't a suitable candidate for Roth IRA conversions.

How Required Minimum Distributions (RMDs) Work While You Are Alive

Unfortunately, you cannot keep money in retirement accounts indefinitely. The SECURE Act extends the age to begin mandatory distributions from IRAs, 401(k)s, 403(b)s, 401(a)s, 457 plans, etc. (which we are generally lumping under the term IRAs) from age 70 (technically April 1st of the year after you turn age 70½) to age 72 (technically April 1st of the year after you turn age 72).

Let's assume you have sufficient income and money outside of your IRAs and that you don't need more money from your IRA than the RMD. Let's assume you want to pay taxes later, but you are required to take distributions from your IRAs. In that case, you should probably limit your withdrawals to the RMD, again unless you are trying to reduce what will become an Inherited IRA because you know that your kids are going to get clobbered with taxes after you die.

Each year after age 72, you must withdraw your RMD by December 31st. Roth IRA accounts are excluded from this requirement—they do not require withdrawals until after the death of the Roth IRA owner and his or her spouse.

In simple terms, your RMD is the minimum amount you must withdraw from your retirement account each year. That income will be added to your taxable income, unless it was contributed on an after-tax basis, or if the qualified withdrawals are tax-free as in the case of the Roth IRA or Roth 401(k).

The point is that just because you are taking minimum distributions and Social Security, don't assume you aren't a suitable candidate for Roth IRA conversions.

Your RMD is calculated by dividing the balance of your IRA or retirement account by a distribution period (or factor) found in IRS Publication 590. Table 3 (also called the Uniform Lifetime Table) applies if you are married and your spouse is NOT more than 10 years younger than you, or if your spouse is not the sole beneficiary of your IRA, or if you are unmarried.

Table 1 would only be used to calculate your RMDs if you inherited an IRA from someone other than your spouse. If you are married and your spouse is more than 10 years younger than you and the sole beneficiary to your IRA, you would use Table 2 – Joint Life and Last Survivor Expectancy.

Most of you who are reading this book will probably use Table 3. Effective 2021, the Table 3 distribution period (or factor) for your first RMD at age 72 is 27.3. (That is a change from the old law but isn't part of the SECURE Act. We include it because it is relevant. Please see the section below "New Regulations Are Part of the Mix.")

It doesn't matter if you're in perfect health and that both of your parents lived to be 100. Table 3 is based on the government's estimate of the joint life expectancy of the IRA owner and someone deemed 10 years younger than the IRA owner. The following is an oversimplification and isn't technically accurate, but it is easy to remember. If you're 72, the government assumes under the new life expectancy factors that you are going to live for roughly 17 more years, and then tacks on another 10 years to determine the Lifetime Table life expectancy factor. So, let's look at how your first RMD will be calculated.

Start by looking at how much money you had in your IRA as of December 31st of the previous year. To keep the math simple, I'm going to assume that you had exactly $1 million. To calculate your first year's RMD, divide the $1 million by the factor that for this example I will assume to be 27.3 for a 72-year old IRA owner from Table 3. $1 million divided by 27.3 equals $36,630. That's how much you have to withdraw from your IRA, and how much additional income will be added to your other existing income.

Here's another way of looking at it. Your first RMD at age 72 will be right around 4% because the 27.3 divisor is a little larger than 25. Were the factor 25, it would be 4% exactly. And as you age, the distribution period that you must divide into your IRA balance gets smaller, which means you are required to take out ever larger RMDs. If you have $1 million in your IRA at age 90, your distribution period is only 12.1, which will cause an RMD of $82,644.63!

These forced withdrawals cause headaches for many seniors, not just because they are taxable distributions but because they have an impact on your entire tax return. The distributions can throw you into a higher tax bracket, increase the percentage of taxable Social Security benefits, and raise your Medicare B and D premiums. But, notwithstanding the problems you face when you are forced to withdraw money from your retirement plans, the advantages of years of tax deferral far outweigh the disadvantages of not saving money in the tax-deferred environment.

Please note that Table 2, used if your spouse is more than 10 years younger than you, gives you a much higher divisor resulting in a lower RMD and a lower tax. Why else would Hugh Hefner of Playboy fame marry a woman 60 years his junior? He wanted to lower his RMDs and cut his taxes! Great tax planning, Hef!

Additional details about these rules and a description of how your RMD is calculated based on your life expectancy factor can be found in IRS Publication 590-B, available online at **www.irs.gov/pub/irs-pdf/p590b.pdf**.

The SECURE Act doesn't make any changes to the RMD rules while you and/ or your spouse are alive. The new legislation will keep the same basic format as above but will defer the time you have to take your first minimum distribution until age 72. This change is actually one of the few things that is welcome in the new law. It will allow additional time for tax deferral and will likely allow an additional two years during which Roth IRA conversions will be beneficial to you and your family.

As with the old law, you will always be allowed to take out more than the minimum, but if you can afford to limit your distributions to the minimum, there are significant financial advantages, as represented in the graph above. Limiting distributions to the minimum defers taxes on the IRA for the longest time available and, subject to exceptions, confers the greatest financial benefits.

Special Rule for Qualified Plan Owners Who are Still Working Past Age 72

Generally, RMD rules apply to traditional IRAs and qualified plans (401(k)s, 403(b)s, etc.). The rules governing 401(k)s and 403(b)s, however, have one nuance that might be extremely important (in contrast to the rules for IRAs). If you are still working after age 72, the IRS does not require you to take a distribution from the retirement plan connected to your current job as long as you do not own more than 5% of the company.

I have a lot of college professor clients who continue to work at their long-time university job well past age 72. They often just keep deferring their 403(b) distribution RMD until they retire or die. That strategy worked better before the SECURE Act because their families weren't penalized when they left their large retirement plan to the next generation. But, under both the old and new law, that is an option for those working past 72.

New Regulations Are Part of the Mix

Near the end of 2019, the Treasury Department passed proposed regulations expected to be finalized by January 2021 that will add roughly a year and a half of life expectancy under the Uniform Life Table. So, a 72-year-old will have a factor of 27.3 rather than the life expectancy under the current tables of 25.6. Since that doesn't change the big picture that much, we will not be covering the details of that proposed regulation.

So, now that we have an overview of some of the basics of saving and spending retirement assets, let's look at how the legislation governing IRA distributions at death worked in the past and how it works now. Understanding how the "stretch" distribution rules worked in the past sheds valuable light on why the "death of the stretch IRA" is such a terrible blow to your estate plan. It is important for you to understand both how the stretch worked in the past, and how it works now. Please read on.

KEY IDEAS

- Pay taxes later, except the Roth.
- Use a Health Savings Account if one is available to you.
- Use employer provided matches to your retirement plan.
- Contribute to Roth IRAs and your Roth 401(k) while you are working.
- Spend your after-tax dollars before your IRA.
- Most individuals should try to limit withdrawals from retirement accounts to the minimum required by law (RMD).

Defeat the "Money Worries" Triggered by COVID-19

In addition to the dangers of infection, the coronavirus can also make you sick by burdening you with more stress and worry, specifically about health, and perhaps even more so, money.

For example, when the stock market plunged nearly 25% on Black Monday (October 19, 1987), California's hospital admissions spiked by more than 5%[3].

More recently, on March 16, 2020 worries about the coronavirus caused the Dow to fall 2,997 points—the biggest one-day drop ever, producing worry and stress in countless investors[4].

Money worries can literally make you sick: Nearly one-third of participants in an American Psychological Association survey said stress impacts their physical or mental health. Physical symptoms of stress include low energy, nausea, aches, pains, chest pain, and many more[5].

---

[3] https://en.wikipedia.org/wiki/List_of_largest_daily_changes_in_the_Dow_Jones_Industrial_Average
[4] https://www.usatoday.com/story/money/2020/02/27/dow-markets-plunge-correction-coronavirus/4889977002/
[5] https://www.webmd.com/balance/stress-management/stress-symptoms-effects_of_stress-on-the-body#1

One way to relieve stress from money worries, and the illness financial distress can cause, is to let a professional worry about your money for you.

When **Lange Financial Group** manages your IRA and retirement plans, we help you get the most out of what you've got—no matter what's going on with the economy, the markets, or the world.

That way, Lange Financial can help relieve the burden of money and retirement worries, so you can sleep soundly at night.

To protect your legacy wealth for greater peace of mind, call Lange Financial right now toll-free at **1-800-387-1129** or go to **page 175**. So, you can stop worrying all the time and start living again.

$$2$$

What Happens to Your IRA When You Die?
A Look at the Contrast Between the Old Regulations and the SECURE Act

"Certain things, they should stay the way they are. You ought to be able to stick them in one of those big glass cases and just leave them alone."

— J.D. Salinger, *The Catcher in the Rye*

First, A Look at what Remains the Same

Let's start with a simple case. You are married, and if your IRA beneficiary form is completed properly (it often isn't) and there is appropriate estate administration after your death (there often isn't), your IRA will likely pass to your spouse as the primary beneficiary. Your spouse can transfer your IRA into her own IRA, using a technique called a spousal rollover. We would prefer that she make the transfer using a different technique called a trustee-to-trustee transfer.

The trustee-to-trustee transfer electronically moves the funds from the decedent's IRA or retirement account directly to the surviving spouse's IRA avoiding the potential mix up and withholding tax problems caused by cutting a check. This trustee to trustee technique assuming it is done right, eliminates the possibility of horrendous tax consequences caused by human error of the spousal rollover. This was true before the SECURE Act, and it is still true.

If you were taking RMDs from your IRA before your death and your spouse is roughly your age, she must continue to take RMDs from your IRA (which has now become her IRA via the trustee-to-trustee transfer). Her RMDs will be similar to the ones you received because they will also be based on a joint life expectancy. This time, though, it's the joint life expectancy of your spouse and the life expectancy of someone deemed 10 years younger that determines her RMD. There are other rules that apply to spouses who are more than 10 years younger than you, but we will not cover them here. You can read about them in Chapter 5 of my book, *Retire Secure!*, which you can get by for free by going to **https://paytaxeslater.com/books/** or purchasing a copy from Amazon.

At least with the old law and depending on your situation even with the SE-CURE Act, it is likely to your spouse's advantage to continue to defer the taxes and take only the RMDs from the IRA for as long as possible. The benefits of doing so are illustrated in Chapter 1, where we show the advantage of keeping the money in the IRA while spending after-tax money first. But what happens after both spouses are gone or one spouse "disclaims" (we will explore disclaimers more in Chapter 5) to the children or grandchildren? This is where the intense pain of the SECURE Act should strike terror in the hearts of IRA and retirement plan owners.

Under the old law, if your beneficiary was a child or grandchild, or any non-spouse beneficiary for that matter, any or all of them could have "stretched" the Inherited IRA over their lifetimes. (An IRA that is inherited by a non-spouse beneficiary becomes a special asset called an Inherited IRA.) The RMD for the Inherited IRA used to be calculated by dividing the balance in the Inherited IRA as of December 31st of the previous year by the life expectancy of that beneficiary. Even though they were required to begin taking taxable distributions from an Inherited Traditional IRA the year after their parents or grandparents die (the

beneficiary of an Inherited IRA is not permitted to defer distributions until age 70 ½ or 72 under the SECURE Act as the original owner did), the RMDs were much smaller than the RMD of the original IRA owner because of the child's/ grandchild's much longer life expectancy. These rules allowed your Traditional IRA to continue to grow tax-deferred *for a very long time.*

Required Minimum Distribution Under the SECURE Act

Under the SECURE Act, an Inherited Traditional IRA, subject to exceptions, must be fully distributed and taxed by December 31st of the year that includes the tenth anniversary of the IRA owner's date of death. This causes a massive income tax acceleration, and many lost years of income tax-deferred growth.

In the case of an Inherited Roth IRA, the distributions to the beneficiary are not taxable because the original Roth IRA owner paid the taxes. Inherited Roth IRAs continue to grow income-tax free. Under the old law, the Roth IRA beneficiary could "stretch" the tax-free distributions over his or her life expectancy, similar to an Inherited Traditional IRA.

Under the SECURE Act, an Inherited Roth IRA, subject to exceptions, must be fully distributed within 10 years of the Roth IRA owner's death. This doesn't cause a massive income tax acceleration, but it does mean the beneficiary is losing many years of income-tax free growth that was available to him under the old law. Further, this means ten years after the death of the Roth IRA owner, any dividends, interest or realized capital gains will be subject to income tax just like a regular taxable investment.

And while you might not think that the old mechanism for stretching an IRA was all that important, these rules allowed IRA owners to create family tax-deferred and tax-free dynasties that ultimately provided lifetime incomes in the millions of dollars to their children and grandchildren. Even on a smaller scale, it allowed children of IRA owners to have a lifetime of income that was a valuable supplement to their own income. Now it will be much harder to leave that kind of legacy to your heirs through your retirement accounts.

As recently as 2019 we had, unfortunately but inevitably, a number of clients die. Some with more than $2,000,000 in IRAs and some with substantial Roth IRAs. Children of clients who died in 2019 had enormous opportunities for income tax deferral. We had a death in the last few days of 2019 and, while both Matt (our estate attorney) and I were genuinely sad, we both had the same thought—much better that he died before year-end than after year-end. Going forward, children will have fewer opportunities.

Table 2.1, at the top of the following page demonstrates why it was advantageous to inherit an IRA under the old law. It assumes the beneficiary elects only to take RMDs from the Inherited IRA. In the table, the first year is the RMD of the IRA owner who died at age 80. His 45-year-old beneficiary must begin taking an RMD from the Inherited IRA the year after the owner's death when he is age 46. To save space, we skipped some middle years and picked up towards the end of the beneficiary's life. Look at the bottom line…

New Regulation (Not the SECURE Act) for Pre-2020 Deaths for Non-Spouse Beneficiaries

Nothing is ever simple. Though it is favorable, to add to the complications, there were other regulations that changed the life expectancy factors and created new tables that reflect the divisor that will be divided into the balance in the account as of December 31st of the prior year to establish the required minimum distribution of the inherited IRA. The higher the life expectancy factor (the divisor), the lower the RMD of the inherited IRA.

Please note this regulation was in addition to the SECURE Act and reflects a slightly longer life expectancy.

You need to look at the beneficiary's age in the year after the IRA owner's death under the new tables and subtract by one for each subsequent year until the current year. Here is an example.

Technical Example that Most Readers Can Skip...

- Charles Sr., age 85 died in 2014 leaving his son, Charles Jr., age 54, as the beneficiary of his IRA. Per the regulations, Charles started taking distributions in 2015 based on his age that year (i.e., 55). The divisor for someone 55 years old in 2015 was 29.6. Under the single life expectancy provision, a non-spouse beneficiary reduces his divisor by one each year when calculating his RMD (i.e., the reduction method). Under these conditions, in 2021 his divisor would be 23.6.

- Under the proposed regulations, his divisor is recalculated in 2021 using the new Single Life Expectancy Table starting with the revised factor for the age he began taking RMDs (i.e., 55) and subtracting one for each year of distributions. Therefore, he would start with a factor of 31.5 and subtract six years resulting in a divisor of 25.5 for 2021. Compared to the current regulations, the divisor will increase which will reduce Charles Jr.'s RMDs and will generate less taxable income for

TABLE 2.1
Old Law for IRA Distributions
Old Law – Inherited IRA Distributed Over Lifetime

YEAR	AGE	INHERITED IRA BALANCE	ANNUAL DISTRIBUTIONS	TOTAL DISTRIBUTED
2020	*80*	*$ 1,000,000*		
2021	46	$ 1,063,566	$ 26,132	$ 26,132
2022	47	$ 1,074,284	$ 27,060	$ 53,192
2023	48	$ 1,084,468	$ 28,022	$ 81,214
2024	49	$ 1,094,066	$ 29,020	$ 110,234
2025	50	$ 1,103,025	$ 30,055	$ 140,289
2026	51	$ 1,111,287	$ 31,128	$ 171,417
2027	52	$ 1,118,791	$ 32,242	$ 203,659
2057	82	$ 471,136	$ 100,242	$ 1,994,933
2058	83	$ 390,216	$ 105,464	$ 2,100,397
2059	84	$ 301,514	$ 111,672	$ 2,212,069
2060	85	$ 203,815	$ 119,891	$ 2,331,960
2061	86	$ 94,870	$ 101,511	$ 2,433,471
2062	87	—	—	**$ 2,433,471**

2021. Most IRA experts are considering the proposed regulations in their RMD calculations now even though the regulations are not scheduled to be effective until 2021.

What Happens to Your IRA When You Die Under the SECURE Act?

With the new 10-year rule for distributing an Inherited IRA, the beneficiary could take zero distributions for the first nine years after the death of the parent or grandparent but then, he or she would have to take out the entire amount in the tenth year but that would likely push the beneficiary to the top income tax bracket. So, for this example (please see Table 2.2 on the next page), I treated the distributions to come out more evenly. Look at the bottom line…

TABLE 2.2
IRA Distributed Under the SECURE Act
SECURE Act – Inherited IRA Distributed Over 10 Years

YEAR	AGE	INHERITED IRA BALANCE	ANNUAL DISTRIBUTIONS	TOTAL DISTRIBUTED
2020	*80*	*$ 1,000,000*		
2021	46	$ 927,500	$ 142,500	$ 142,500
2022	47	$ 849,925	$ 142,500	$ 285,000
2023	48	$ 766,920	$ 142,500	$ 427,500
2024	49	$ 678,104	$ 142,500	$ 570,000
2025	50	$ 583,071	$ 142,500	$ 712,500
2026	51	$ 481,386	$ 142,500	$ 855,000
2027	52	$ 372,583	$ 142,500	$ 997,500
2028	53	$ 256,164	$ 142,500	$ 1,140,000
2029	54	$ 131,595	$ 131,595	$ 1,271,595
2030	55	—	—	**$ 1,271,595**

Though it really isn't exactly an apple-to-apple comparison, please note that in this example the beneficiary inheriting under the old law received $1,161,876 more money than the beneficiary under the new law. Please see detailed assumption for both tables in the Appendix.

Please also note in the table above, I have assumed that the beneficiary chooses to take the distributions evenly over the 10-years. In reality, the best time to take a taxable withdrawal from a Traditional Inherited IRA would be when your beneficiary is in their lowest tax bracket, as long as it is within 10 years of the death of the IRA owner. So, if a beneficiary is perhaps in medical school and in a low tax bracket but is likely to be in a much higher tax bracket after graduation, internship and fellowship, then the beneficiary should consider taking more taxable distributions earlier.

Subject to exceptions, if the beneficiary of a Roth IRA doesn't need the money currently, they should just let the inherited Roth grow income-tax free for 10 years after the death of the original Roth IRA owner. To oversimplify, if the beneficiary inherited $1,000,000 in a Roth IRA and the money is invested at 7%, he will have a $2,000,000 account in 10 years. Again, the distributions from that account are not taxable, but dividends, interest and realized capital gains will be taxable after the 10-year period after the money in the inherited Roth IRA becomes a plain after-tax brokerage account.

Obviously, the new law governing post-death RMDs for most non-spouse beneficiaries is not advantageous—in fact, it is disadvantageous.

This massive income tax acceleration, which is what I have spent much of my career trying to help people avoid, is exactly what the law wants to accomplish. The effects will be devastating to your heirs if you have a substantial IRA—unless you act to make significant changes to your retirement and estate plan. One of the reasons the SECURE Act bothers me so much is that it dramatically reduced my legacy of at least a billion dollars of IRA and Roth IRA funds that would have otherwise been deferred by one, two, or even three generations costing my clients and readers billions of additional tax dollars.

Planning for the Small Stretch that Survived is Still Critical

At this point, let me also add this cautionary note. Even with its diminished value, taking advantage the 10-year limited stretch is still important. Unfortunately, the "stretch IRA" is botched far more often than it is done right.

Someone, whether it is the attorney, the advisor, the CPA, or the client, usually makes a mistake that destroys the stretch IRA, causing a major tax acceleration for the beneficiary. For example, if Dad dies leaving his IRA to Junior and the advisor titles Junior's Inherited IRA as "Junior, IRA," the ability to stretch the IRA is lost forever and, consequently, Junior suffers a major tax acceleration. The correct name for the account is "Inherited IRA of Dad for the Benefit of Junior." If you don't have the magic language in the new account title, or don't do exactly as you should in many other ways, your heirs will be taxed—literally and figuratively.

To realize the "stretch IRA," however limited, you need appropriate estate planning and appropriate estate administration after the death of the IRA owner. This was true under the old and remains true with the new law. Please note there are special "stretch" opportunities for minors and disabled or chronically ill beneficiaries that should be considered.

What if the Beneficiary of the IRA or Roth IRA is a Trust?

If the end beneficiary is a trust, there are technical requirements that the trust must meet to be deemed a designated beneficiary and for the trust to receive the "stretch IRA" status. Please see pages 307-308 in *Retire Secure!* for a list of conditions that the trust must meet. Otherwise, the trust suffers enormous income-

One of the goals of a special needs trust is to provide money to the beneficiary, but not in such a way as to interfere with any type of government benefit that the beneficiary may be receiving or might receive in the future.

tax acceleration, too. Please note that many attorneys, banks, and even CPAs are touting the benefits of "IRA Trusts." They typically name the bank or financial institution as trustee. Subject to exceptions, I prefer to name a family member as trustee. You can achieve the same tax result by having it drafted by the appropriate attorney, but still have the advantage of a family member as trustee. The advantages of a family member as a trustee or even executor for that matter are typically lower fees and keeping control in the family.

Remember exceptions to the 10-year rule are offered for disabled or chronically ill beneficiaries. More often than not, money left to such a beneficiary should be left in a special needs trust. One of the goals of a special needs trust is to provide money to the beneficiary, but not in such a way as to interfere with any type of government benefit that the beneficiary may be receiving or might receive in the future.

The drafting of this trust that is named as the beneficiary of your IRA, will, as it has in the past, require special language to protect the beneficiary's government benefit, but also to minimize the income tax implications. This means if you have a beneficiary with a disability or chronic illness, it is critical to have the trust for the beneficiary drafted by an attorney who not only understands the consequential language needed for a special needs trusts to allow beneficiaries to continue to qualify for government benefits, but also understands the right language to qualify as a designated beneficiary to the pre-2020 lifetime stretch for the trust. Though our law firm has that expertise, we are only licensed to practice law with Pennsylvania residents. We can, however, help residents from most other states with developing a financial masterplan and managing investments.

Another obvious trust situation is to name minor children as beneficiaries as a trust. Remember, minor children of the deceased IRA owner only (and not other minors) are partially exempted from the income tax acceleration rules. Under current law a minor child (or a trust for a minor child) may "stretch" the Inherited IRA or Roth IRA as under the old law up until the minor child reaches the age of majority. (Likely 18 or 21, depending on the residency of the minor, 18

"Retire Secure Initial Consultation" — yours FREE!

On January 1, 2020, the SECURE Act took effect. It now forces your IRA and other retirement plans to be fully distributed and taxed within 10 years of your passing.

As a comparison between Table 2.1 and 2.2 shows, this accelerated taxation can mean a difference of more than $1.1 million in total distributions to your heirs. So, if you are reading this, but have not done anything about it yet, much of the wealth you worked so hard to earn during your lifetime may be taxed away.

But now, as an owner of this book, you may qualify for a FREE, no-obligation **Retire Secure Initial Consultation** (value: $997) introducing you to proven tax-saving strategies—including Roth IRA conversions, gifting, **Lange's Cascading Beneficiary Plan**, life insurance, CRUTs, sprinkle trusts, asset allocation, and more—to keep your legacy wealth in your family's hands ... and out of Uncle Sam's. All 100% legal, so it won't raise an eyebrow at the IRS.

To qualify for a *Retire Secure Initial Consultation*, you must have $1 million or more of investable assets that you would consider placing under management with **Lange Financial Group**—assuming you like our retirement planning and tax-saving strategies as well as our money manager and his process.

Our "standard operating procedure" was to consult with clients in our Pittsburgh offices. But to help keep you healthy as well as wealthy, we are, for a limited time, doing these free initial consultations remotely via phone or Zoom. That way, there's no travel. No cost. And you get a tax-smart "second opinion" on your retirement planning—all at a safe social distance, in the comfort of your own home.

There is no cost for your initial consultation. It's yours free of charge. For more information or to schedule your free *Retire Secure Initial Consultation*, call us toll-free today at **1-800-387-1129**.

in Pennsylvania). At that point, the 10-year clock starts ticking. But, if a 10-year-old inherits an IRA, they could have between 18 and 21 years of income tax deferral.

So, it is crucial that the trust be drafted appropriately.

Accumulation Trusts *vs.* Conduit Trusts and the Potential Need to Redraft your Trusts

Typically, accumulation trusts are permitted to accumulate income inside the trust. This might be appropriate if the income from the trust exceeds the needs of the beneficiary and the trustee doesn't want to give the beneficiary more money that he or she needs (or the owner of the IRA wants to keep total control over the money from the grave)! So, while the trust does not have to pay out all the RMDs from the IRA to the trust beneficiaries, distribution amounts not paid are taxed at trust tax rates (generally higher).

An accumulation trust still falls within the 10-year income tax acceleration requirement of the SECURE Act. The advantage of the accumulation trust after the SECURE Act is that the trustee will have more discretion over when and how, during the 10-year term after the death of the IRA owner, as well as after the 10 years has passed in order to distribute income and principle. For instance, if a beneficiary is in college and has little or no income, a good time to distribute income would be before the beneficiary graduates from school and hopefully gets a job that will put the beneficiary in a much higher bracket.

A conduit trust, however, requires the trustee to distribute all the income from the trust. In the example of the college student who might do better to receive money prior to graduation, the trustee of a conduit trust has no control over the timing of the payout. If a conduit trust is named as a beneficiary of the IRA, all the RMDs from the IRA must be paid to the trust and then from the trust to the trust's beneficiaries who pay tax at their income tax rate (avoiding the high taxes on undistributed RMDs). Many conduit trusts with an IRA as the underlying asset were drafted to avoid the high income-tax rates if the money was just left in the trust.

Now, conduit trusts must be re-examined because even though they avoid the high trust tax rates, with the loss of the lifetime stretch any control the IRA owner was trying to exert will be moot both during the 10 years and after 10 years when the law requires that the balance in the inherited IRA must be distributed. The trustee may want to keep money in the trust for the same reason that the trust was set up in the first place. That might include protecting the money from a spendthrift beneficiary, creditor protection, to preserve a government benefit, to protect a beneficiary from a no-good spouse, etc. In those cases, and more, a trustee might not want to distribute the remaining balance of the trust within 10 years of the IRA owner's death. If you want to give the trustee options for more control, and if your current trust is a conduit type trust, that alone might be a good reason to review your wills and trusts and possibly add a codicil or redo at least a portion of your estate plan.

In our office, we are in the process of examining all the trusts we have drafted to serve as the beneficiary of an IRA. In many cases, we will be contacting our clients and recommend they redo their documents. We are ranking them in importance and notifying the clients with the most time sensitive and important situations first.

For example, here is a situation of an estate plan we drafted that includes a trust that urgently needs attention. Assume a spendthrift trust is the primary beneficiary of a multi-million-dollar IRA and the beneficiary of that trust would buy a new guitar before he would pay the rent. Then assume that the spendthrift trust is a conduit trust and the IRA owner is old and sick. That is an urgent situation that needs short-term attention.

On the other hand, if we have a conduit trust that is for the benefit of young grandchildren that are the second contingent beneficiary of an IRA after the spouse and the children, that might not be as pressing. If there isn't a lot of money in the IRA and both the spouse and the children have significant needs, perhaps that estate plan doesn't merit spending any time and money to amend. Of course, I presented the two extremes and most of our clients are somewhere in between.

The point, however, is if you have a conduit trust as the beneficiary or even the contingent beneficiary of your IRA or retirement plan, you may need to update your wills, trusts, and beneficiary designations of your IRAs and retirement plans.

The unfortunate news is that most attorneys botch the basic rules for drafting the trust to qualify as a designated beneficiary that would allow the trust. So, you probably should have your documents redone not because they need to be updated, but because they were never right in the first place. Roughly 90% of the wills and trusts and IRA beneficiary designations with trusts as the beneficiary or contingent beneficiary of the IRA that we review need to be redone not because they are dated, but because they were never done right in the first place.

It should be noted that our law firm is licensed to only practice in Pennsylvania so we can't draft documents for non-Pennsylvania residents. On the other hand, we know what language you need to have the stretch IRA and whether your documents have the conduit trusts as beneficiary of the IRA regardless of your state residency.

KEY IDEAS

- If the largest asset in your estate is your IRA or retirement plan, the beneficiary designations of your IRAs and retirement plans are the most important estate document you have. Please be sure the beneficiary designations on all your retirement accounts are filled out appropriately.

- The SECURE ACT does not change the surviving spouse's ability to rollover or do a trustee to trustee transfer of an IRA inherited from a spouse.

- Subject to exception, the surviving spouse should continue to limit withdrawals to the RMDs for as long as possible.

- Taking advantage of the 10-year limited stretch is still critically important.

- If your IRA is the underlying asset for a trust, you should think about reviewing the trust with an estate attorney who understands drafting trusts when the underlying asset is an IRA or retirement plan.

- Conduit trusts, that were a reasonable choice in the past, should probably be redrafted to protect the beneficiary.

3

The Impact of the New Law

"One moment you appear to be riding the crest of a wave,
only to have the rug pulled away from you, bringing you
back down to earth with a sickening thud."

— **John Barrow**

Congress is Accelerating Taxes on Your IRA After You Die

The new legislation is a money grab by Congress. They are picking the pockets of IRA owners who played by the rules to plan for their heirs. For years, non-spouse beneficiaries could "stretch" Inherited IRAs after the death of the IRA owner. Many employees and retirement and IRA owners planned accordingly and invested as much as they could in their retirement plans, figuring it would be a great tax-advantaged way to accumulate money for themselves and pass money on to the kids. Then, late in the game, Congress, assuming they even knew what they were voting for, decides they need a quick infusion of money, so they change the rules. The impact is devastating for most children and grandchildren of IRA owners. If tax rates go up, and after the CARES Act, I can't see how they will not, the impact of the SECURE Act will be even more devastating. I wrote a detailed peer-reviewed article on an earlier proposed version of this legislation, which was published in the prestigious journal, Trusts & Estates. But I will give you a summary of the details below.

The New Law for Children (or Any Non-Spouse) Inheriting IRAs and Roth IRAs

An IRA that passes to a non-spouse beneficiary is a special asset called an Inherited IRA. Under the SECURE Act (subject to exceptions that we explore in the next chapter) an Inherited IRA will have to be totally disbursed within 10 years of the death of the IRA owner. Period.

If the inherited IRA is a Traditional IRA, the income from the distribution of the inherited IRA will be added to the beneficiaries' existing income and will be taxed at the higher rate, possibly at the current highest tax rate of 40% not including state income taxes. If your beneficiary is a resident of New York or California or another state that taxes IRA distributions and has a high tax rate, taxes for your beneficiary become particularly miserable.

In the case of inherited Roth IRAs, your children won't have to pay taxes on the distributions because distributions from Roth accounts are tax-free. If they can afford it, they should keep the distributions to the minimum and allow the Inherited Roth IRA to continue growing income-tax free for the full 10 years. Please note this is a completely different strategy from what a beneficiary should do when they inherit a traditional IRA.

After the 10 years are up, all the future taxable income on that money will be subject to the full complement of taxes—income, capital gains, etc. That's a big change—the idea that inherited Roth IRAs could compound over many years and distributions (which could be limited to the minimum amount required) would be tax-free was a huge benefit for your heirs. The party is over. In short, this law is miserable for your heirs. They will be taxed aggressively and losing the full stretch will be devastating for them. It's a raw deal.

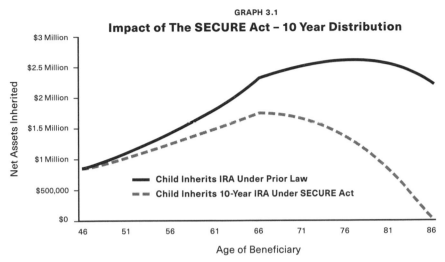

GRAPH 3.1
Impact of The SECURE Act – 10 Year Distribution

Please see detailed assumptions in the Appendix.

Quantifying the Difference Between the Past and the Current Law

Graph 3.1 above represents the impact of the new law governing Inherited IRAs. This graph shows the difference between inheriting $1 million from an IRA that could be "stretched" over a lifetime (solid line) consistent with the pre-2020 law *vs.* a child who inherits $1 million that is subject to the 10-year rule (dotted line).

What this graph is saying is that under the new law given certain assumptions, if you die and leave your IRA to your 46-year-old child when your child is 86 years old, he will be broke. Under the old law, he would have had more than two million dollars. That's a monumental difference.

The only difference between these two scenarios is when the beneficiary pays taxes. Of course, under the old law, the younger the beneficiary, the greater the "stretch."

The impact of leaving an IRA and/or Roth IRA to grandchildren is radically different under the new and old laws. Graph 3.2 on the next page shows the difference of a grandchild inheriting an IRA under the old law versus under the SECURE Act.

The solid line depicts what would have happened if the IRA was left to a grandchild, and the grandchild stretched the distributions over 55 years. The dotted line shows what happens now that the grandchild is required to accelerate the distributions and hence accelerate taxes on the inherited IRA. Even though

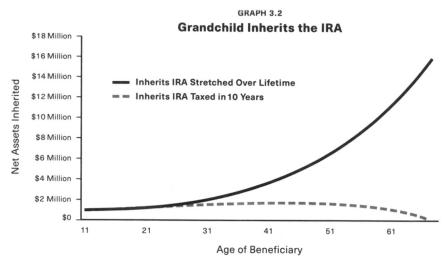

GRAPH 3.2
Grandchild Inherits the IRA

Please see detailed assumptions in the Appendix.

in both cases the grandchild immediately reinvests the withdrawals into a taxable brokerage account, the difference in her wealth by the time she reaches age 70 is an astonishing $16,245,105!

Now that you understand the gravity of the situation and why I find it such a deplorable change for most IRA owners, let's read on to see what we can do about it, including the best defense against the SECURE Act tax grab: combining multiple strategies.

KEY IDEAS

- An IRA that passes to a non-spouse beneficiary is a special asset called an Inherited IRA.

- The SECURE Act mandates that an Inherited IRA must be totally disbursed within 10 years (subject to exceptions).

- Under the new law, if you don't take aggressive action, your legacy will be decimated.

- Providing for your children will be much more difficult.

- Luckily, there are strategies that will make an enormous difference.

In the coming chapters you will learn about:

- the advantages of a flexible estate plan that will protect—even overprotect—your spouse while also providing for an enormous amount of flexibility,
- the advantages of a Roth IRA conversion while you are alive to protect your children from the SECURE Act,
- Social Security strategies,
- charitable strategies,
- gifting strategies,
- asset relocation strategies, and
- the best response—a combination of strategies.

"Retire Secure Initial Consultation" — yours FREE!

On January 1, 2020, the SECURE Act took effect. It now forces your IRA and other retirement plans to be fully distributed and taxed within 10 years of your passing.

As a result, so much of the wealth you worked so hard to earn during your lifetime can be taxed away in one brief decade—robbing your heirs of the legacy wealth you wanted them to have.

But now, as an owner of this book, you may qualify for a FREE, no-obligation *Retire Secure Initial Consultation* (value: $997).

This invaluable free advisory session introduces you to our most effective tax-saving strategies, including Roth IRA conversions, gifting, **Lange's Cascading Beneficiary Plan**, life insurance, CRUTs, sprinkle trusts, asset allocation, and more.

Our advice and methods can help keep your money in your family's hands ... and out of Uncle Sam's. All 100% legal, so it won't raise an eyebrow at the IRS.

To see whether you qualify* for a FREE *Retire Secure Consultation* with **Lange Financial Group** via phone or Zoom, call us toll-free at **1-800-387-1129** or go to **page 175**.

* You must have $1 million or more of investable assets that you would consider placing under management with Lange Financial Group—assuming you like our retirement planning and tax-saving strategies as well as our money manager and his process and investments.

But we urge you to hurry. At the moment, I am the one doing the consultations and I can only offer so many "virtual" *Retire Secure Consultations*. And appointments are made with prospects who are a good fit for our services and after that on a first-come, first-service basis. Once my schedule is filled with *Retire Secure Consultations*, you may have to wait longer than we'd both like or risk not getting an appointment at all.

4

Critical Exceptions to the SECURE Act

"A rule without exceptions is an instrument capable of doing mischief to the innocent and bringing grief, as well as injustice, to those who should gain exemptions from the rule's functioning."

— **Derrick Bell**,

The first tenured African American Professor
at Harvard Law School

Classes and Categories of Exempt Beneficiaries:

Surviving Spouses

As we have said, the new law doesn't apply to your spouse. He or she will still be able to do a spousal rollover or a trustee-to-trustee transfer of your IRA. This is by far the most important exception and thank goodness they didn't change the rules for spouses inheriting IRAs and retirement plans.

Individuals with Chronic Illnesses or Disabilities[6]

Also exempt from the 10-year acceleration of income taxes are individuals with chronic illnesses or disabilities. Though this exception has no impact on the majority of IRA and retirement plan owners, it is crucial to protect individuals with chronic illnesses or disabilities. I have provided some guidance in the foot-

---

6 Please see the bottom of pages 52 and 53 for a full explanation of this footnote.

notes as to what constitutes being disabled. Frankly, I think the definition that the IRS uses to determine who is disabled is far too limited. Parents of a child with a disability have enough challenges in their lives that they should not have to worry about meeting the IRS's strict view of who qualifies as being disabled.

I think that when it comes down to it, if you are "IRA heavy" and don't have substantial after-tax dollars and you want to provide for a beneficiary with a disability, you can use two different strategies or possibly combine both strategies.

The first, is to do everything you can to make sure your beneficiary receives the necessary designation as disabled and then have the appropriate trust drafted when the beneficiary with the disability has an interest in the special needs trust. This option is enhanced if you make a Roth IRA conversion and your beneficiary can get all the benefits of tax-free income for their entire life just like under the pre 2020 rules.

The second is to cash in some IRA money and buy life insurance and make a special-needs trust the beneficiary of the life insurance policy. That would eliminate the worry about the massive income tax acceleration if the beneficiary doesn't qualify as disabled for the purposes of the exception to the ten-year income tax acceleration. It is also a safe alternative.

What has to happen under the new law for a beneficiary with a disability to qualify for the exception to the ten-year acceleration of income taxes? First, you must have appropriate estate planning and more specifically, you must have the

---

6 **Disabled Beneficiary**: A disabled heir is defined in Code Section 72(m)(7): *"For purposes of this section, an individual shall be considered to be disabled if he is unable to engage in any substantial gainful activity by reason of any medically determinable physical or mental impairment which can be expected to result in death or to be of long-continued and indefinite duration. An individual shall not be considered to be disabled unless he furnishes proof of the existence thereof in such form and manner as the Secretary may require."* This definition is quite limited. An heir that a plan holder wants to benefit must have substantial health challenges and have limited earning capacity because of it. However, if the heir can engage in "any substantial gainful activity" even if very limited, that heir will not qualify for this benefit. Thus, the terminology in the definition alone will restrict the applicability of this provision.

Note from Jim: The other issue IRA owners should worry about is that the beneficiary with a disability may not be inclined or able to prove their disability. That is a frequent problem when it comes to proving disability for other benefits like Social Security Disability Income (SSDI). If you have a beneficiary with a disability who you would like to enjoy the benefits of deferring your IRA over their lifetime, it would be prudent to establish proof of their disability while you are still alive.

Chronically Ill Beneficiary: A chronically ill heir is defined in Code Section 7702B(c)(2) with certain modifications. This Code Section provides: *"(A) In General — The term "chronically ill individual" means any individual who has been certified by a licensed health care practitioner as — (i) being unable to perform (without substantial assistance from another individual) at least 2 activities of daily living for a period of at least 90 days due to a loss of functional capacity, (ii) having a level of disability similar (as determined under regulations prescribed by the Secretary (in consultation with the Secretary of Health and Human Services) to the level of disability described in clause (i), or (iii) requiring substantial supervision to protect such individual from threats to health and safety due to severe cognitive impairment. Such term shall not include any individual otherwise meeting the requirements of the preceding sentence unless within the preceding 12-month period a licensed health care practitioner has certified that such individual meets such requirements. (B) Activities of daily living For purposes of subparagraph (A), each of*

correct language for assigning the beneficiary of your IRA and retirement plan. You also must have the beneficiary certified as disabled or chronically ill.

Remember, in this and practically all cases when we are talking about an IRA or retirement plan asset, the key document is *not the will or revocable trust*, but the beneficiary designation of the retirement plan.

There is a book's worth of material on the topic of providing for a beneficiary with a disability or chronic illness. So, with the caveat that I am not being complete, let's discuss some of the major elements.

There is a very good chance that it would be most prudent to leave the money to the beneficiary in a "special needs trust" rather than leaving them the money directly. There are conflicting definitions in the literature about what a special needs trust is, so for the purposes of this chapter, I am talking about a very specific type of trust.

If the beneficiary has a disability or a chronic illness, there is a reasonable chance that either now or at some point in the future, the beneficiary will qualify for some type of government aid. It might be Supplemental Security Income (SSI), Social Security Disability Income (SSDI), Medicaid, or another essential federal or state public benefits program.

The goal of the special needs trust is to make sure that trust is not considered an *available asset* as defined by public benefit agencies. The attorney drafting

---

the following is an activity of daily living: (i)Eating. (ii) Toileting. (iii) Transferring. (iv) Bathing. (v) Dressing. (vi) Continence."
Note from Jim: I would offer the same caution that I mentioned in the previous section on beneficiaries with disabilities. I think it is prudent for you to establish proof of your beneficiary's chronic illness while you are still alive.

The definition "chronically ill" suffers from the same overly restrictive terms as the definition of "disabled" on page 52. Many intended heirs are living with challenges that may limit or even prevent gainful employment, but they are not so severely incapacitated as to meet the requirements of chronically ill according to the above definition. Yet, these same people who need the protections of a trust, and who may desperately need the economic benefits from the plan assets to be bequeathed, will be forced to have the plan balance distributed in 10-years and lose the continued tax deferred growth, etc.

Any plan holder planning on an heir meeting the requirements of being "disabled" or "chronically ill" to qualify as an EDB under the SECURE Act should carefully evaluate the stringent requirements involved.

Additional Rules for Chronically Ill or Disabled Beneficiaries: There is additional leniency permitted to chronically ill or disabled beneficiaries. A trust can be created for their benefit that has multiple beneficiaries. If on the death of the plan holder that trust is divided into separate trusts for each beneficiary, the post-division trust for the chronically ill or disabled beneficiary will qualify as an EDB for life expectancy payout treatment. Without this change each of those separate trusts for each beneficiary would have to have separately been indicated to be a beneficiary.

Also, in contrast to a spouse or minor child who require a conduit trust to qualify for the special life expectancy payouts as EDBs, a chronically ill or disabled heir can be the beneficiary of an accumulation trust as well. Even though the accumulation trust may name beneficiaries on the death of the chronically ill or disabled beneficiary the chronically ill or disabled beneficiary will be permitted to withdraw pursuant to the life expectancy rules rather than the 10-year payout. **https://pay taxeslater.com/secure-act-planning-ideas-martin-shenkman**

the trust must be mindful of both income and principle when drafting the trust because too much of either, without the appropriate provisions, could result in loss of benefits or potentially the requirement to return benefits.

Over the years, competent attorneys who work in this area have found language that works for these purposes. Ideally, the person drafting the trust to be named as the beneficiary of an IRA or retirement plan would keep in mind the rules to protect the beneficiary's government benefit, and also to preserve the "stretch" of the inherited IRA. This provision is particularly important if the IRA and retirement plan is the primary asset in the estate.

In my practice, I have seen IRA owners try to get around all these complications by naming a sibling as the beneficiary of the IRA or other funds for that matter with the tacit assumption that the sibling will use the money for their brother or sister with a disability and not themselves.

This might work, but it could also be disastrous. What if the named beneficiary falls victim to a lawsuit, bankruptcy, or a divorce and loses the money that was intended for their sibling with a disability? This work-around is not on our list of recommended strategies, even though it might work.

The other problem with this approach is that only the beneficiary with the disability or chronic illness can stretch the inherited IRA so this "oral trust" approach is a particularly bad idea under the SECURE Act when the underlying asset is an IRA.

Finally, even if the trust is drafted perfectly, having a lot of IRA or retirement plan money in this type of trust is far from ideal. We discuss life insurance in Chapter 12 and for a lot of reasons having a life insurance policy owned by a special needs trust for the benefit of the beneficiary is likely at least part of a good solution to provide for the long-term financial security of a beneficiary with a chronic illness or disability.

Other Exceptions to the 10-Year Rule

There are two other exceptions to the income-tax acceleration in 10 years rule.

1. Beneficiaries who are not more than 10 years younger than you are not subject to the 10-year income acceleration. The two most likely beneficiaries that aren't more than ten years younger than you are unmarried partners and siblings.
2. Charities and charitable trusts.

Unmarried Partners

Let's assume you are planning to leave at least a portion of your IRA or retirement plan to your unmarried partner. The good news is that the partner will be able to use his or her life expectancy factor under the single life expectancy tables as the divisor to determine the RMD for the inherited IRA which is consistent with the old (pre-2020) law. But it is still much worse than leaving that IRA to a married partner.

First, if you marry and then die, your spouse could take a required minimum distribution not only based on their life expectancy, but also the joint life expectancy of themselves and someone deemed 10 years younger than them. This would allow a much greater deferral or stretch IRA than if you died and left your IRA or even a portion of your IRA to your partner.

This could also have implications on the estate of the unmarried partner. The beneficiaries of your partner, which could be your beneficiaries too, would likely be able to receive a much longer tax deferral if you were married.

I would suggest if you have a significant other and you would at least consider getting married, please consider the financial implications. They could be enormous, and in most cases advantageous. The advantages will be even greater under the SECURE Act.

Let's assume you are in a committed relationship but not married. Let's further assume you are much stronger financially than your partner. If you get married and if you predecease your partner, there will be income tax advantages, estate and inheritance tax advantages, that could be substantial. Even if you don't plan on leaving your partner any of your money, without any cost to you, you could significantly protect your partner's income with your Social Security benefits.

Let's assume you have a high earnings record for Social Security and are receiving a benefit of $3,500 per month. Your partner, though a terrific person, only receives $1,000 per month. If you get married, while you are both alive your partner would get a big raise that could be in the ballpark of an extra $500 per month. But more importantly, if you predecease your partner, when you die your partner could, subject to exceptions, get your benefit of $3,500 per month for the rest of your partner's life.

So, even if you wanted to leave all or most of your money to your children or other members of your biological family, you could go a long way towards

> **I would suggest if you have a significant other and you would at least consider getting married, please consider the financial implications. They could be enormous, and in most cases advantageous.**

protecting your partner financially in a way that would not have any impact on the family money.

Of course, I would still recommend a prenuptial agreement. Also, please be aware I am only scratching the surface of the topic "getting married for the money." Though dated and specifically geared for same-sex couples, the principles discussed here can be found in a book I wrote called, **Live Gay, Retire Rich**, a book that I wrote before same-sex couples could be legally married in all fifty states. In that book I talked about getting married in a state that allowed same-sex marriages for the financial benefits of getting married and then moving back to the state you reside in. I am considering writing an updated version. If I did, I would not limit the audience to gay couples. The books title could be *"Get Married for the Money."* The point is if you are in a committed relationship, and you are considering getting married, you should consider the financial implications and the ability to protect your partner/spouse.

Charities and Charitable Trusts

Charities and charitable trusts are a critical exception to the 10-year income acceleration rule for IRAs and retirement plans.

The charitable trust exception will create enormous opportunities for many readers, even if you are not particularly charitably inclined. We include an entire section on charitable trusts in Chapter 8. There are new advantages to naming a charitable trust as the beneficiary of your IRA. Along with two other strategies for charitable giving with IRAs and retirement plans also covered in this book, my goal is to move a billion dollars to charity and still have your children receive more money.

Leaving Money to a Sibling

As mentioned earlier, beneficiaries who are not more than 10 years younger than you are not subject to the 10-year income acceleration. In addition to unmarried couples, this exception will likely have an impact if you want to provide money to a sibling. This exception will help them provided that the surviving sibling's life expectancy under Table 1 is more than 10 years.

Challenges for Blended Families—Providing for the Surviving Spouse and Leaving Money Equitably to Children

Let's assume that you were married, had children, got divorced or lost your spouse, and married someone else. Let's assume the same is true for your second spouse. In that situation it is natural to want to at least partially if not fully provide for your second spouse, but at his or her death, to have whatever is left go back to the children of your first marriage, not to the children of your second spouse.

If the underlying asset *is not an IRA* and the amount is large enough to justify the costs of drafting and maintaining a trust, a trust as beneficiary may work out fine. The trust could read something like income to spouse, principal distributions if needed for health, maintenance and support, and when your second spouse dies, the remaining money in the trust goes to the children from the first marriage. That protects your spouse and makes sure anything from you that is left after your second spouse dies goes back to your children. Your second spouse could have a similar trust but with you as the income beneficiary. This is nothing new and there are different variations of this type of trust. Many attorneys refer to it as a marital trust and we have drafted many of them in our practice. I often prefer a simpler solution of x percent to spouse and the rest to children of the first marriage. But, with after-tax dollars, the trust is not necessarily an ill-fated solution.

But what if the underlying asset *is an IRA*? The trust described in the above solution becomes an income tax disaster.

Many IRA owners and even estate attorneys start their planning by thinking about how to divide the pie (the entire estate) among the different beneficiaries at their death. I prefer to think about how to make the biggest pie and after I figure that out, then I try to cut it up to achieve the approximate allocation to the different beneficiaries that the client has in mind.

This is critically important and frankly a very different solution from the one offered by most estate attorneys. For example, I just met an elderly couple facing the exact situation; it was a second marriage for both of them and they both had children from a former marriage. We were enjoying a particularly scenic sunset in Tucson, Arizona. Perhaps we should have been talking about how beautifully the sunset lit the mountains and was still glowing on the clouds. But we weren't. Somehow, we started talking about their estate plan.

They had the types of trusts I mentioned above *but* they also had the issue that virtually all the underlying assets were held in IRAs. This meant that after the first death, instead of getting the favorable stretch allowed for a surviving spouse inheriting a spouse's IRA, there would be a massive income tax acceleration after the first death. The required minimum distributions for these trusts are very high and would spark the acceleration of income taxes which would hurt the surviving spouse and the children of the first spouse to die. This was a lousy plan under the old law and under the SECURE Act, it is especially miserable because of the 10-year rule. The only winner with that estate plan would be the IRS.

The solution that their estate attorney drafted would yield a particularly bad result because they didn't have extra money available. Let's assume they each had $500,000 in their respective IRAs and not much else. With two $500,000 portfolios and two Social Security benefits, the couple will have sufficient means to support a decent lifestyle, if not an extravagant one.

If they had a lot more money, or if they had pensions, they could each leave a certain amount or percentage to the other and the rest to their respective children. That way they would be providing for their surviving spouse and their children from the first marriage without the complications or disadvantages of the trusts. The taxes, even if not reduced to what they could have been, would be manageable.

The problem with them having a lesser amount is that if they don't provide for each other, the lifestyle of the surviving spouse may be threatened. In addition, if they decide to leave some of their IRA to each other and then the rest to the children of the first marriage, they could have a terrible result because the surviving spouse might not have sufficient funds to maintain their lifestyle. If they tried to estimate how much money will be left and what the needs of the surviving spouse would be, they could be wrong.

There is so much uncertainty in the portfolio performance, future laws, future needs, etc. A "certain percentage" or even a certain amount might be insufficient depending on a situation we can't predict. What if we were drafting documents in December 2019 that provided a certain percentage to the spouse. Then, assume the first death was after COVID-19 which caused a huge drop in the market. The plan of leaving a certain amount or percentage could easily force a compromised lifestyle for the surviving spouse.

Many IRA owners and even estate attorneys start their planning by thinking about how to divide the pie (the entire estate) among the different beneficiaries at their death. I prefer to think about how to make the biggest pie and after I figure that out, then I try to cut it up to achieve the approximate allocation to the different beneficiaries that the client has in mind.

If they leave everything to each other, then the children of the first spouse to die won't get anything and the children of the second to die will get everything which isn't what the couple wants. But, trying to figure out how much to leave the children and each other in this situation is a tough guess. You either risk under providing for the surviving spouse, or if you leave too much to the surviving spouse, you could underprovide for the children of the first spouse to die.

This couple's attorney drafted the types of marital trusts that I could live with if the underlying asset is not an IRA. (Income to spouse and at that spouse's death, to children of first marriage.) But when the underlying asset is an IRA, their plan is an income tax disaster for both the surviving spouse and the children from the deceased spouse's first marriage.

I often encounter this situation or something close to it in practice. I should mention that the solution that I am going to recommend or at least suggest considering is frowned upon by other estate attorneys and one of the top estate attorneys in the country that works with blended families is likely shaking his head as he is reading this.

Granted, my recommendation will not be advisable for every couple, absolute trust between them is very important. I begin by asking one spouse if they completely trust the other spouse. If I get a yes without hesitation, I ask the other spouse the same question. Again, assume I get another yes.

Let's begin by looking at the easy case when the assets between the two couples are roughly equal and dividing the pie at the first death would threaten the lifestyle of the survivor. Under those circumstance, I suggest that instead of drafting a trust, that each spouse names the other as the primary beneficiary of their IRA or at least a major portion of the IRA. Then, and here is the key, they both name the children of both marriages (50% for his children, 50% for her children) as the contingent beneficiaries. That way, the surviving spouse will be provided for no matter who dies first. Assuming there is no change in the estate plan after the first death, the children from both marriages will eventually get whatever is left—half to his family and half to her family. The income taxes saved through implementing this plan (which incidentally is a demonstration of the advantages of paying taxes later), could ensure that the surviving spouse is secure and comfortable and the kids from both spouses receive a tax-savvy inheritance after both spouses are gone.

I recognize my illustration is simple with both spouses having an equal amount of money—that doesn't frequently happen in my practice. But I think you can see the logic. In my scenario you get a much better tax result because no one would suffer the massive income tax acceleration that both generations would suffer under the martial trust scenario.

I suggest that instead of drafting a trust, that each spouse names the other as the primary beneficiary of their IRA or at least a major portion of the IRA. Then, and here is the key, they both name the children of both marriages (50% for his children, 50% for her children) as the contingent beneficiaries.

The reason this alternative is frowned on by the profession is that many estate attorneys harbor the legitimate fear that the surviving spouse would change the beneficiaries of, what is now the surviving spouse's IRA, to his or her children to the exclusion of their spouse's children.

As I mentioned, trust is a big variable. I address this problem by recommending that both spouses sign contracts agreeing not to change the beneficiaries of their IRA in a way that would harm the interest of the children of the first spouse to die.

Yes, there is certainly a chance that either an unscrupulous surviving spouse or even a third-party could take advantage of the situation. I don't want to diminish that possibility. But sometimes you have to weigh the risk of unscrupulous behavior versus massive income taxation where the only sure winner is the IRS. By the way, if I had reason to suspect the contract would be violated, I would look for a different solution. No contract is likely to protect the innocent party if the other person is unscrupulous.

Of course, the decision does not rest with me. Each couple has to decide. But when I have suggested this, most of my clients in this situation prefer to enjoy the certain tax savings, even risking unscrupulous behavior by their spouse. That said, we still draft and have both spouses sign a contract saying they won't change their documents after the first death in a way that would hurt the children of the first marriage. The old Russian proverb often attributed to Ronald Reagan applies here: "Trust but verify."

So, while the trust offers protection against an unfair result in terms of who gets what, you are guaranteed a bad tax result. With my solution, the contract offers some protection, but also offers a much better tax result.

Please note that is consistent with our general approach to retirement and estate planning. First, let's figure out how to make the biggest pie. (In this case the formal trust method guarantees massive income taxes and the pie is made smaller by the accelerated taxes.) After we figure out how to make the biggest pie, then we worry about dividing it.

Unfortunately, even after I discussed this issue with the strolling couple, the husband said he thought they should go back to the estate attorney who drafted the trusts for them. In my opinion, that is the wrong response. Don't go back to the estate attorney who drafted documents that almost guaranteed a bad result. Even under the old law, the two marital trusts were a lousy plan guaranteed to pay high taxes. It would be better for this couple to find an estate attorney who understands the issues and hopefully has experience drafting documents in these situations.

Matt Schwartz, our lead estate attorney reports that roughly 90% of the trusts that are drafted when the underlying asset is an IRA or retirement plan are not drafted correctly and the consequences can be severe. Matt offers another advantage, unlike the vast majority of estate attorneys, he has a Math degree from Northwestern and is particularly good at solving more complicated situations. It is totally baffling to me that even high-priced estate attorneys with excellent reputations consistently botch the handling of trusts when the underlying asset is an IRA.

Please note, much to my chagrin, we are only licensed to practice law in Pennsylvania because theoretically we aren't "competent" to practice law in other states. So, the totally green guy who graduated last in his class from law school, but somehow managed to pass the bar exam on his third attempt, is deemed competent to draft these complicated estate plans in his state, but our firm is not. Please forgive my grousing…

As a practical matter, if we get an out-of-Pennsylvania assets-under-management client and we aren't happy with their estate plan, though we don't draft it ourselves, we try to find and/or work with an estate attorney licensed in their state.

What if the Spouses in the Second Marriage are Not Financially Equal?

For the last seventeen years, I have presented various retirement and estate planning seminars for the Westinghouse SURE Group, a group made up, primarily, of retired Westinghouse engineers. Most recently, one guy in particular, came up to talk with me after the program. He was very open about his financial situation. He had a substantial IRA as well as money outside his IRA. Both he and his second wife had children from prior marriages. He was much stronger financially than she was. They had a prenuptial agreement.

He bragged to me that between him and his high-priced downtown attorney (not me), they developed a plan where he was going to name his children as the beneficiary of his IRA and leave the money he already paid tax on to his wife.

Let's even assume he worked out the numbers so that plan comes close to cutting the pie between his wife and his children the way he wants.

I probably should have let it go, but I didn't. I knew it wouldn't be easy to convince this stubborn guy he was wrong. But again, I thought he was data driven.

The plan he described creates a smaller pie for his wife and the children of his first marriage. Under the SECURE Act, leaving IRA money to a spouse will allow a lot more tax deferral than leaving IRAs to adult children. So, the first part of his masterplan starts with accelerating taxes for his children. I suggested that he leave at least a portion, and probably a substantial portion of his IRA to his wife and the after-tax dollars to his children. That switch of who gets what would have significantly reduced the tax burden on both his spouse and his kids. His objection to that idea was that it would give more to his wife than he wanted and not enough to his children.

So, if we used my suggestion of leaving more money in his IRA to his wife, we had the problem of how to cut the pie after making the bigger pie. With the numbers in this case, we needed to provide more value to the kids, even if down the road.

I suggested that his wife sign a contract similar to the one presented above but the contract would state whatever money she inherits from him she agrees to keep separate from her other monies. She also agrees that at her death that whatever is left from that separate account that was originally funded with his IRA will go to his children. It would also be possible to put in a provision that if his wife takes out a required minimum distribution from an IRA that she inherited from him, that after paying the taxes, should would be required to invest that money back in a pot that would eventually go to his children.

There could also be spending limitations or suggestions for "his" pot of money.

The reason for that limitation is he would not want her to use all his money first while growing her own money and leaving her own money to her kids.

Ultimately, the goal is to make the pie bigger and cut it up in a way that would satisfy the IRA owner. My proposed solution of leaving more IRA money to the spouse and having her leave that money to his children approximates the spirit of the marital trust, but without the massive income tax acceleration. By the way, even before the SECURE Act, I hated marital trusts as the beneficiary of an IRA and now find them despicable.

Again, I would never do this "trust your spouse" plan if either member of the couple didn't completely trust his/her second spouse. As I mentioned earlier, it isn't foolproof. But, if we can save hundreds of thousands of dollars in taxes or in some cases seven figures by making a bigger pie, it should at least be considered.

The good news was the engineer, even though he thought he knew more than he did—and more than me—was data driven. (You might notice that I have had multiple experiences with engineers having to be persuaded with numbers— I guess it comes with the job, and I have some personal experience with it as my wife, Cindy, has a master's degree in electrical engineering from Carnegie Mellon University.)

If you are in a second marriage with children from a prior marriage and you have a significant IRA and you want to provide for both your spouse and your children, we encourage you to "run the numbers" to see which way will work out better in the long run for both your spouse and your children. Consider the contract that I described above.

Disclaimer: I warned of the potential problems with this strategy and though I have a general disclaimer in the beginning of the book, this strategy could blow up. You should see appropriate estate attorneys and number crunching CPAs and understand the risks and benefits of this strategy before acting.

Again, the big picture lesson is start by making the biggest pie for the family by minimizing what goes to the IRS so there is more for the everyone else. Then, figure out how to cut it.

Leaving IRAs and Retirement Plans to Minor Children

Most readers of this book are more likely to have minor grandchildren than children, but this information may be useful for some, including your children. Another critical exception for planning purposes, though only a partial exception, applies to minor children of the IRA owner who have not yet reached the age of majority—the age of majority varies from state to state but the range would be 18 to 21-years-old. Once reaching the age of majority, however, the 10-year rule kicks in. Since the Act does not define the age of majority, some commentators believe it may also include children under the age of 26 who are enrolled in a specified course of education, which could extend the age of majority five to eight years. Once reaching the age of majority, which is usually either 18 or 21 (18 in PA), the 10-year rule kicks in.

So, let's assume you are planning on leaving a portion of your IRA to your child and you die unexpectedly when the child is five years old, and you live in a state that sets the age of majority at age 18. After your death, your child would get a significant income tax deferral between five years old and 18 years old. He would be taking a required minimum distribution of the Inherited IRA based on his life expectancy consistent with the pre-2020 law. After he reaches 18, (and for the moment assume the exception of waiting until age 26 doesn't apply), he would then get an additional 10 years of tax deferral. So, that child could take advantage of 23 years of income tax deferral which could be enormous.

Obviously, if you leave money to a minor child, subject to exceptions, you will likely want to have a well drafted trust as the beneficiary of your IRA or retirement plan with the minor child as the beneficiary of that trust. Again, you have to get the trust drafted correctly. The trust must meet five specific conditions in order to get the maximum stretch that is still available. In addition, the trust must be handled appropriately during the estate administration period and for that matter until 10 years after the minor child reaches their majority. Matt Schwartz, our veteran estate planning attorney, estimates that roughly 90% of the trusts he sees for minors are deeply flawed when the underlying asset is an IRA or retirement plan. Please see p. 307 of *Retire Secure!* for an enumeration of the conditions and a deeper explanation of what happens if the conditions aren't met.

This minor's children exception to the income tax acceleration of the SECURE Act is another reason why a variation of Lange's Cascading Beneficiary Plan might be an excellent choice as the beneficiary of your IRA and retirement plan. Please see Chapter 5.

KEY IDEAS

- The surviving spouse is the most important exception to the 10-year acceleration of income after death as legislated in the SECURE Act.

- When providing for beneficiaries with disabilities or chronic illnesses, be extra vigilant with respect to appropriate estate planning and the correct language for assigning the beneficiary of your IRA and retirement plan.

- If you have a partner but are unmarried, think about the long-term tax and Social Security advantages of getting married.

- Charities and charitable trusts are excepted from the 10-year income acceleration rule for IRAs and retirement plans which create enormous opportunity for IRA owners even if they aren't that charitable.

- If you are leaving money to your minor children, you will probably want a well drafted trust that includes the five specific conditions to get the best tax treatment.

5

The Best Estate Plan for Most Married IRA and Retirement Plan Owners After the SECURE Act

"Blessed are the flexible for they will not allow themselves to become bent out of shape."

— **Robert Ludlum**

Choosing the Right Beneficiaries for Your Retirement Plan

What follows is one of the most important facts in this book: *Your will (or your trust documents, if you have them)* **do not** *control the distribution of your IRA after your death.* Any account that has a specific beneficiary designation will be distributed to the individuals who are listed on the beneficiary designation form, regardless of what your will or trust says. In other words, the beneficiary designation of the IRA trumps the will (no pun intended, sorry about that. I am a bridge player and a small trump beats an ace in any suit except the named trump suit).

In my practice, clients often come in with sophisticated wills or trusts that were drafted with every possible contingency in mind. They might be 30 or 40 pages long and come in a big notebook binder. When I ask them where most of their money is, they usually reply "in my IRA" or "in my retirement plan." Then when I ask them about the beneficiaries of their IRAs and retirement plans, I find that, despite all of the time and money they've spent on these wills and trusts, the beneficiary designation form that controls the majority of their wealth is filled out with just two simple lines:

- Primary Beneficiary: *My Surviving Spouse*
- Contingent Beneficiary: *My Children Equally*

This simple beneficiary designation, while better than nothing, is nowhere near optimal. I hate it when I have to tell new clients that they have spent a lot of time and money on complicated estate plans that, after they die, will not accomplish the family's goals because the beneficiary designations that they have listed on their retirement accounts were not part of a coordinated and integrated estate plan. Unfortunately, the difference between effective and ineffective planning can mean the loss of hundreds of thousands, sometimes millions, of dollars for your heirs. By the way, the problem with the simple beneficiary designation existed before the SECURE Act, but the SECURE Act will potentially compound the problem.

The Elephant in the Room of Estate Planning

The elephant in the room with estate planning is uncertainty. As of December 31, 2019, we had a radically different law governing Inherited IRAs and retirement plans than we do today. As we go to press the S&P is down about 10%–this all happened in a few short months. Uncertainty is a given.

In 2019, we had quite a few deaths of clients with IRA and retirement plans of over a million dollars, and the outlook for many of their families is radically better than if they had died just one year or in one case, one week later. That is because we used the disclaimer concept and had money going to children and grandchildren on the first death.

If a client died after March 2020, we would not have the income tax incentive to disclaim IRA dollars and in addition, with a 10% drop in the S&P, the surviving spouse would rightfully be more hesitant to disclaim.

The point is there is a constant uncertainty surrounding what laws will be in effect when you die. You can't control Congress or the market or many other things.

By the way, I tried. I set up a website and a Facebook page called "Save our Stretch" that provided information and also included easy directions to write your Congressional representatives explaining how unjust killing the stretch IRA was. You can see where that got us. I think from now on, I will stick to trying to get the best result for my readers and clients without trying to get the law changed. Who is to say the law won't be changed at least one more time before you die, or perhaps multiple times with multiple changes?

Investment performance and future spending are also unpredictable. Perhaps a terrible and expensive illness strikes either you or your spouse and everything that is left is needed for the surviving spouse. An alternative and more positive scenario would be that the market goes up, and there is a lot of money left after the death of the first spouse. At that point, it might make sense to have at least some of the money go to children or grandchildren at the first death—this is where it gets more complicated with the new legislation.

Fundamentally, we don't know what the future tax laws will be. We don't know now what will be going on with your family at the time of your death. Our firm has done thousands of long-term projections. What all the projections have in common is they have all been wrong, or at least off-base. Something different happened from what we thought would happen. *That doesn't mean you shouldn't do projections and act on the course that seems best suited to your situation.* It is to say, however, that accurately predicting family circumstances, the tax laws, the market, etc. is nearly impossible. It is one of the reasons we conduct annual strategy reviews (in addition to the reviews the money manager does) to account for unforeseen (or for that matter foreseen) changes.

Furthermore, for each type of asset, whether it is an IRA, a Roth IRA, a brokerage account, life insurance, an annuity, a house, or other asset, there might be compelling reasons for who should get what both at your death and when your spouse dies. To make it more complicated, a change in circumstances could change the optimal choice of which beneficiary gets which asset.

If your estate plan includes traditional estate planning documents that "fix in stone" the distribution of your assets to your heirs, they are not likely to get the full benefit of your legacy. Better decisions regarding who should get which assets can be made after your spouse dies, when circumstances are current and clear. Furthermore, if your estate planning documents are drafted in accordance with the principles of **Lange's Cascading Beneficiary Plan**, your surviving spouse will have nine months after your death to think about options and determine the best strategies both for themselves and the family.

These decisions can be made either with their family or, ideally, with their family and a trusted advisor who understands the enormous benefit of flexible estate planning combined with tax-savvy post-mortem estate planning. Post-mortem estate planning is when you determine a course of action based on what

---

If your estate plan includes traditional estate planning documents that "fix in stone" the distribution of your assets to your heirs, they are not likely to get the full benefit of your legacy.

---

is best for the spouse and the family after the death of the IRA owner. Similarly, after you both die, providing your heirs (usually children) with as much flexibility as possible is also optimal. So, what can you do to give yourself and your heirs maximum flexibility?

What follows assumes a "Leave it to Beaver" family. Perhaps I am dating myself. If you don't understand the reference, it refers to a couple who have been married once, to each other, and they only have children from their union. This means both of them have the same ultimate beneficiaries which is likely some combination of children and grandchildren. This is the old-fashioned traditional family unit (like mine).

There are other planning strategies that come into play with different circumstances. Different strategies are called for if you are in your second marriage and have children from your first marriage or if you have a love child from the sixties who is not the child of your spouse, or one of countless other variations. But, for now, let's examine the optimal plan for the traditional family. We are also going to assume your primary goal is to provide for your surviving spouse. Leaving money to children and grandchildren is usually a secondary goal.

So, given these assumptions, what if there was an estate plan that could help you can save hundreds of thousands or even millions of dollars for your family? What if you could get money to your children when they need it most? Or when they could make better use of the money than if they have to wait for the second spouse to die. What if you could do all that while still protecting your surviving spouse, doesn't that seem like the best solution?

Lange's Cascading Beneficiary Plan (LCBP)

Starting in the mid-nineties, I began adding additional flexibility to our traditional wills and trusts and to the beneficiary designations of IRAs and retirement plans. At the time, this was pretty much unheard of. In 1998, I described my plan in *The Tax Adviser*, the peer-reviewed journal of the American Institute of CPAs. An adaptation of that article is available by going to **https://pay taxeslater.com/reading/roth-iras-accumulating-tax-free-wealth/**. The peer reviewers loved the plan and actually had me expand my description of the plan even though the primary subject was Roth IRA conversions. (Incidentally, that article won article of the year and was the first peer-reviewed article on Roth IRA conversions.)

Then in 2001, immediately after a change in the law passed that enhanced the values of "disclaimers" (read on) I received explosive coverage for the strategy that I called Lange's Cascading Beneficiary Plan (LCBP). The recommendations I made in the 1998 article, which I implemented in the wills, trusts, and IRA beneficiary plans that I was drafting for my own clients, now proved to be of greater value than when I first started drafting them.

The concept was groundbreaking, and since then, I have been quoted many times on the topic in national publications such as *The Wall Street Journal* (multiple times), *Newsweek, Kiplinger's, Financial Planning, Trusts & Estates*, and many others. The concept takes complete advantage of stretching IRAs to their fullest—when I developed the plan the "fullest" was over a lifetime, now it is 10 years—which benefits the heirs of IRA and retirement plan owners. The idea is simple but is intended to save you and your heirs a lot of time and money.

If it's set up properly, LCBP can give your heirs an enormous amount of flexibility. Under the LCBP, your surviving spouse can make decisions based on his or her own needs, the needs of the family, how much money is left, the type of assets that are left, the tax laws that are in effect at the time of your death, etc. Furthermore, your spouse has nine months from the time of your death to make those decisions.

An Explanation of the Best Estate Plan for Most Married Couples with Traditional Family Structures

My plan is as simple as this. Start by naming primary and contingent beneficiaries to your IRAs and retirement plans (and possibly most if not all the other assets) according to the following hierarchy:

1. your spouse,
2. your child (or children equally) as the contingent beneficiary or beneficiaries,
3. the grandchildren, though likely in a trust depending on their ages. There would be a separate trust for the children of each of your children.

Perhaps the best description of my plan from a noted source comes from *Kiplinger's* in 2001.

Lange paints this scene: You are married with children and grandchildren. You name your wife as the primary beneficiary. The first contingent beneficiaries are your children equally. The second contingent beneficiaries are trusts for your grandchildren. Each set of grandchildren has their own trust. At your death, your wife could roll over all or part of the IRA into her IRA. Your wife could also disclaim a portion, which would be distributed to your children. Finally, if neither your wife nor your children need all of the money, they could disclaim all or a portion to a trust for the grandchildren.

The key concept here is "disclaiming." You can't force anyone to accept a bequest. My plan allows the beneficiary of the IRA (or of any assets if you set it up that way) to accept the IRA for him/herself, or to say, "I don't want that IRA or I don't want part of that IRA." If there is a "disclaimer" of all or part of an IRA, we look to see who is next in line, or if we want to use the official term, the contingent beneficiary. The ability for the primary beneficiary to make a "partial disclaimer" adds enormous flexibility to the plan. This means that he or she can accept part of the asset and let the contingent beneficiary have the rest.

Think about how it would work. If your surviving spouse needs all the money, that's fine—he or she can keep everything you left to them. End of story. But if your spouse doesn't need the money, or more likely doesn't need all of the money, then he or she can disclaim either all, or again more likely, a portion of it, in favor of the next beneficiary on the list—your children. If you have two children with unique needs, one can accept the inheritance and the other can disclaim their inheritance, or a portion of their inheritance, to a trust for the benefit of their own children.

I know I said it earlier, but it deserves repeating: each beneficiary down the line can have a partial disclaimer if they want to retain some, but not all, of the Inherited IRA or other asset. Again, I want to give the surviving spouse the option to keep, disclaim, or partially disclaim not only the IRA and retirement plan,

but all other assets including Roth IRAs, after-tax dollars, life insurance, etc. I'd also like to make it crystal clear that the surviving spouse or for that matter the next named beneficiary has the right to disclaim all or part of every asset.

In addition to having specific disclaimer language in the will, revocable trust, and all the beneficiary designations of IRAs, Roth IRAs, etc., this plan anticipates the possibility of your grandchildren inheriting IRAs or other assets even if your children are alive.

With traditional planning and traditional estate administration, the children don't get any inherited money until both of their parents are gone. The grandchildren don't get anything until their parents are gone. Whereas the additional flexibility of LCBP allows children to receive money at the first death which not only has potential tax advantages, but also helps the children out while they are younger.

Usually, the only way a grandchild receives an inheritance is if the grandchild's parent predeceases them. With LCBP, we anticipate the possibility of a grandchild inheriting money while their parent is alive. That gives us the ability to name your children as trustees for the grandchildren.

As long as you trust your spouse to disclaim any part of the inheritance that he or she doesn't need, and depending on things like the market situation at the time of your death which can't be predicted now, and if all of the parties involved understand the reasons for it, disclaiming can not only reduce taxes after your death, but also get money to younger generations sooner when they have greater financial need for it.

Our law firm has drafted 2,769 wills, trusts, and estate plans, and LCBP has played a significant role in most of them. We started drafting them in the mid-nineties. Many of those clients have since died. Having a plan in place that protects or overprotects the surviving spouse and allows flexibility to save taxes or get the appropriate assets to the appropriate beneficiary has enormous benefits.

Using the power of disclaimers will require more strategic thinking with the new legislation. Under the SECURE Act, it might not make sense for the surviving spouse to disclaim a large IRA to a child. Your grown children and grandchildren will pay a steep price because they will have to withdraw everything within 10 years.

So, let's assume you want the maximum flexibility possible for your heirs. You have established a LCBP for your estate planning documents. Now, let's look at how the LCBP can work to your advantage in conjunction with the SECURE Act.

Looking at LCBP in Conjunction with the SECURE Act

Let's assume you die with a large IRA and the documents give your surviving spouse complete discretion as to whether she wants to keep the entire IRA, disclaim part of the IRA, or even have a portion of the IRA pass to a grandchild or grandchildren. Your spouse, presumably with the help of an attorney or the appropriate advisor, assesses her financial position. Let's assume there is more money than she requires, and her own children don't have any need for money. Under the old law and even under the SECURE Act, it might make sense for her to disclaim a portion of the IRA to the children who would further disclaim to the grandchildren to spread some of the income among multiple beneficiaries depending on the tax circumstances of the children and grandchildren.

Perhaps the situation is different. Perhaps the kids need some money after the first death. Their income is low, and they need money and your spouse wants to provide that support. In that case, she could "disclaim a portion of her IRA" and the kids could either cash in their share immediately or better yet, do it gradually over the 10-year period incurring minimal taxes.

Another possibility is that the person to receive the disclaimed asset falls into one of the exceptions discussed above, such as a child with disabilities.

A new use of disclaimers we are exploring is the use of disclaimers to a *sprinkle trust* rather than to children or grandchildren. Sprinkle trusts will be discussed separately.

Also, it often makes sense to do tax projections to assess the impact of different beneficiaries receiving money at various times while always keeping in mind the tax rates for the individuals involved.

Matt Schwartz, our veteran estate planning attorney (who incidentally has a math degree from Northwestern) sees great value in strategically disclaiming a portion of an Inherited IRA to reduce income taxes for the entire family.

Matt thinks there should be a focus on the 24% tax bracket. This means that the surviving spouse could project his or her income if they were to accept the entire IRA. If that amount would put them in the 32% bracket (between $163,301 to $207,350 for single taxpayers in 2020) or higher, they could disclaim an amount so that they would not exceed the top of the 24% bracket which in 2020 is between $85,526 to $163,300.

Although there is no guarantee that these historically low tax rates will remain after 2025, and if I were a betting man I would say they are more likely to go up, it seems advantageous to consider taking advantage of the lower income tax rates through strategic disclaimers.

For example, let's assume there is a 74-year-old surviving spouse and two adult children. Let's assume her new projected income if she were to accept the entire IRA would be $203,000. That income exceeds the top of the 24% bracket for a single individual and pushes her into the 32% tax bracket by $40,000. If she were to disclaim about $1,000,000 of her spouse's IRA, her annual income would then be reduced by $40,000 to $163,000 which is the income level at the top of the 24% tax bracket for a single individual. Her annual income would be reduced by $40,000 because if she had kept that $1,000,000, based on her life expectancy factor under the new life expectancy tables (which would be approximately 25 years) she would have been required to withdraw 4% of that $1,000,000 balance.

To simplify, let's assume each kid spreads their portion of the $1,000,000 distributions over ten years and let's assume that that extra income will be taxed at 24%. By doing that strategic disclaimer, we saved the family 8% (32% minus 24%) on $1,000,000, or $80,000.

Matt suggested calling this strategy the *24% Optimizer Tax Strategy*. Maybe he shouldn't be so modest. Maybe we should call it the *Schwartz 24% Optimizer Tax Strategy*. Of course, Steve Kohman and Shirl Trefelner, our veteran number crunchers, have been calculating strategic disclaimers for years. But they never articulated it like Matt, so they don't get to have their name on it!

To oversimplify, the goal of the *Schwartz 24% Optimizer Strategy* and similar strategies is that with savvy post-mortem planning, we can lower tax rates for the entire family on the inherited IRA withdrawals and save the family a lot of money.

The Increased Importance of the Step-Up in Basis Rule Under the SECURE Act

I have been recommending a variation of the following strategy for years, but it takes on a new importance with the SECURE Act. I recently met with a prospective client, and I had proposed a number running engagement for $7,500. He wasn't sure he would receive that much value from working with us. Then, I told him about the strategy that follows and how it would save at least $250,000 and all of a sudden, paying $7,500 to come up with tax-savvy strategies didn't seem like very much, and he agreed to the engagement.

Anyway, here it is for you at no cost except the cost of the book.

> **To oversimplify, the goal of the Schwartz 24% Optimizer Strategy and similar strategies is that with savvy post-mortem planning, we can lower tax rates for the entire family on the inherited IRA withdrawals and save the family a lot of money.**

Let's assume you have a million dollars of highly appreciated after-tax stock investments or, better yet, rental real estate in a jointly held account or even a joint revocable trust. It could be any amount for the concept to work.

The status quo is that at the first death, there will be a one-half step-up in basis and by operation of law those funds will go to the surviving spouse, unless special action is taken. (For a discussion of step-up in basis and the law regarding a step-up in basis for joint property, please go to **https://paytaxeslater.com/Gallenstein-Article.pdf** for an article I wrote on the topic in 1994 which is still good law!)

For pre-2020 deaths, if we wanted our children or grandchildren to get money after the first death, we usually recommended "disclaiming" IRA or retirement plan money. We did this because the child or even grandchild would get a much longer stretch and be able to defer income taxes for a lot longer. Now, the surviving spouse is likely to get a greater tax deferral than if the children were to receive the IRA money directly. So, disclaiming IRA money doesn't make as much sense unless there is an income tax savings like under the Schwartz 24% Optimizer Strategy. But, let's say that isn't an option or is only part of the solution. What if we want children or grandchildren to benefit sooner rather than later, and we still want to be smart about taxes?

It is possible for the spouse to disclaim the highly appreciated after-tax assets in a joint account that just got a one-half step-up in basis, but we may have complications and still not have a great tax result. Because of the nature of some types of joint accounts, it may be automatic or encouraged for the survivor to accept ownership of the assets, complicating, at best, or disqualifying, at worst, the ability to make a disclaimer.

Additionally, the method by which the financial institution tracks or records the cost basis may make it impossible to accurately track the one-half step-up in basis if it is not recorded as a separate tax lot, often resulting in an asset with an average of the new one-half stepped-up basis and the existing one-half original basis. In that case, whether it is the parent or child, someone will still have to pay capital gains rates on one-half of the appreciation. It is not impossible to achieve the optimized tax benefits from assets within a joint account, but greater care must be taken than if the assets were held individually.

This strategy is most easily illustrated by an example supposing that instead of holding money in joint name, we separate the million dollars of highly appreciated stock into two $500,000 accounts and transfer $500,000 of highly appreciated stock to each spouse. That way, no matter who dies first, there will be at least one $500,000 account that has a full step-up in basis. The spouse could then either keep that money for him or herself or "disclaim" all or part of it to his or her kids. This result is also possible within a joint account, but the individual account is a much more straightforward process and removes some of the complexity.

This strategy of separating highly appreciated joint property and transferring half to each spouse could add a lot of flexibility to your estate plan. It would likely allow the family to save a lot of money by reducing their capital gains. It could also make it more tax-efficient to get money to the children at the first death without accelerating income as would happen if you disclaimed IRAs. Alternatively, if we have very good reason to believe one spouse will die much sooner than the other, then we would likely transfer that stock to the person who will likely die sooner.

It is important in either case, whether an individual or joint account, that the financial institution tracks the account's cost basis on a per tax lot method and does not utilize an average cost method by default. A separate individual account provides simplicity as there is only one basis to step-up and track when the assets are transferred. It is also important to review the account's options for how to treat tax lots when selling an asset to make sure that you can choose specific tax lots and not operate under a "First In, First Out" or "Last In, Last Out" method of accounting so that you have the most flexibility in controlling capital gains.

If the asset is rental real estate, the strategy of transferring the property from jointly held to putting it in the name of the person who is more likely to die sooner can be enormously beneficial.

Let's assume the surviving spouse wants to keep the property. She could start depreciating it all over again. Alternately, she could sell it and not pay capital gains. Finally, she could disclaim it to her kids, and they could start depreciating it at the fair market value. If we are talking about a piece of fully depreciated property that is valued at $1,000,000 at death, the tax savings of the step up in basis might be worth as much as $240,000. To be fair, you would get $120,000 tax savings if you left it in joint name (one-half of the step up in value). So, that transfer could save the family $120,000 plus the state taxes on the gain.

By the way, I was talking about the potential "death of the stretch IRA" more than five years ago. Here is another prediction of a future tax change: someday, Congress is going to eliminate the step-up-in-basis rules. It will be an administrative nightmare, but they won't care. It will also kill all the projected savings from taking advantage of the step-up in basis rules.

This is the second time in this book when I talk about timing death properly for tax purposes. The best-timed death was that of George Steinbrenner, the late owner of the New York Yankees. He died in 2010, the only year there was no federal estate tax. That meant his family didn't pay any federal estate tax on the transfer of his multibillion-dollar interest in the New York Yankees.

If it had been almost any other team, except perhaps the New England Patriots, it wouldn't have bothered me that much. But I hate to see the Yankees get a billion-dollar tax break!

If you happen to be a dyed-in-the-wool New York Yankees fan, you should know something that virtually every Pittsburgher who is age 50 or older knows. Playing against the Yankees in a tied game in the ninth inning of the seventh game of the 1960 world series, Bill Mazeroski, the second baseman for the Pittsburgh Pirates, hit a home run to win the World Series against the heavily favored New York Yankees. Another fun fact is that, though the seating capacity of Forbes Field was 35,000, there are at least 60,000 Pittsburghers, including my brother, who say they were there that day…sorry for the digression.

In conclusion, I believe that the combination of Lange's Cascading Beneficiary Plan with a focus on disclaimers and some of the sub-strategies like the Schwartz 24% can save families $100,000 or more in taxes.

Forcing 10-Year Payout for Successor Beneficiaries of Existing Inherited IRAs and Future Inherited IRAs

As I mentioned earlier, in 2019 we had quite a few clients who died with IRAs of more than a million dollars. Either by leaving IRAs directly to a child or through a disclaimer, a lot of large IRAs were inherited by adult children.

The good news for those beneficiaries (who inherited IRAs prior to January 1, 2020) is that they will be permitted to "stretch" that Inherited IRA over their lifetime—they will be governed by the laws in place at that time, i.e., before the new rules took effect.

I was talking about the potential "death of the stretch IRA" more than five years ago. Here is another prediction of a future tax change: someday, Congress is going to eliminate the step-up-in-basis rules.

The bad news is that the terms of the old rules only apply to the initial beneficiary. Once you die and if you pass on the Inherited IRA, your heirs will be subject to the 10-year rule. Under the old rules, your beneficiary could have "stretched" the IRA over what remained of your projected life expectancy according to the table, even though you were dead. This is tricky, but potentially important for people who have inherited IRAs before 2020.

Perhaps an example is appropriate. Your dad died in 2018 and left you a million-dollar IRA. You were 50 years old at your father's death and have been taking the required minimum distribution of the Inherited IRA since your dad's death. The new law will not change your "stretch IRA" distribution pattern.

Let's say, however, that you die at 60 and you have named your child as the beneficiary. Under the old law, your child could have stretched the Inherited IRA of the Inherited IRA (that wasn't a mistake) over your official "remaining life expectancy" according to Publication 590. So, your child would use your remaining life expectancy according to the tables, even though you are dead. Under the new law, your children will have to distribute all the proceeds within 10 years of your death.

This entire "Death of the Stretch IRA" is a huge money grab by Congress, and this provision just rubs salt in the wound.

Unfortunately, even your heirs who qualify for exemptions from the accelerated IRA taxation rules will eventually fall victim. For example, once a minor child reaches the age of majority, she will be subject to the 10-year rule. Furthermore, if she dies before reaching the age of majority, then her beneficiaries will be subject to the 10-year rule immediately—even if they are not of the age of majority themselves. The same is true of an individual with disabilities who inherits an IRA. When he dies, his beneficiary must withdraw and pay taxes on the IRA within 10 years. So, while some accommodation is available for individuals with unusual needs and for individuals who have already inherited IRAs under the old law, those privileges will not be extended to their beneficiaries.

Flexible estate planning with Lange's Cascading Beneficiary Plan is just the start of what you can do proactively to protect your family. Let's explore other strategies.

KEY IDEAS

- Your will and trust documents do not control the distribution of your IRA after your death.

- Any account that has a specific beneficiary designation will be distributed to the individuals who are listed on the beneficiary designation form, regardless of what your will or trust says.

- One of the problems with estate planning is uncertainty.

- LCBP builds critical flexibility into providing for your heirs using the concept of "disclaiming."

- Disclaimer planning with LCBP allows the possibility of income tax reduction of $100,000 or more as well as getting money to the younger generations earlier when they most need it.

- Using the power of disclaimers will require more strategic thinking with the new legislation.

- Consider splitting your jointly held investments into a his and hers account to enjoy a 100% step up in basis no matter who dies first.

FREE Estate Plan Review for Pennsylvania Residents

As a reader of this book, if you are a Pennsylvania resident, you are invited to call for a FREE review of your estate plan (value: $500).

It makes good financial sense to periodically review your estate plan, because there is always uncertainty surrounding what laws will be in effect when you die—and you can't control Congress. For instance, in 2020 (the publication date of this book) and going forward, we now have radically different laws governing Inherited IRAs and retirement plans than we did in 2019.

Our veteran estate planning attorneys can review your family situation, list of assets, income, beneficiaries, trusts, wills, and other relevant financial information to evaluate whether you should have your estate plan updated or redone.

At the moment, **Matt Schwartz**, our senior estate attorney, is the person you will talk with initially. Matt may be overwhelmed at some point, but at least for now, he will be your first contact. Until the corona pandemic is less of a concern, all meetings are virtual—phone calls or Zoom conferences online exclusively.

Pennsylvania residents who would like to schedule a free Estate Plan review should call the **Lange Legal Group** toll-free at **1-800-387-1129** now.

Appointments for Estate Plan reviews are made on a first come, first serve basis, so we urge you to respond today.

6

Roth IRA Conversions Before and After the SECURE Act

*"Wise people understand the need to consult experts;
only fools are confident they know everything."*

— **Ken Poirot**

*Now may be the best time in history to do a Roth IRA conversion. This chapter warrants
reading and for many IRA owners, warrants taking action.*

How Roth IRA Conversions Help Reduce Balances in Traditional IRAs

Before we get into the trees, let's start by looking at the forest.

Most people, at some point in their lives, will likely enjoy enormous benefits
through Roth IRA conversions. This was true before the SECURE Act became
law. It was true immediately after the SECURE Act became law, and the potential
benefits of a series of Roth IRA conversions went way up after the market impact
of COVID-19 and CARES.

One of the unifying principles of planning after the SECURE Act is that, subject to exceptions, it makes more tax sense to die with a smaller balance in your
Traditional IRA or retirement plan to minimize the impact of the 10-year rule.
One of the ways to achieve this overriding goal is to make a series of Roth IRA
conversions. For many, if not most, IRA owners, becoming proactive about developing a long-term Roth IRA conversion strategy combined with flexible estate
planning documents and an appropriate low-cost index fund portfolio is one of
the best financial decisions you can make. If your estate is larger than a million
dollars, a series of Roth IRA conversions and gifting may also be appropriate.
This was true before the recent change, and it is still true.

We have written extensively about the benefits of Roth IRA conversions. Though dated, but still quite relevant, we have written a book dedicated to Roth IRA conversions that can be downloaded without cost from my website at **https://paytaxeslater.com/books/**. Though some of the details have changed, the fundamental concepts have not. With a Roth IRA conversion, you pay taxes once and never again.

While Roth IRA conversions have been one of our signature strategies since the Roth IRA was introduced in 1998, our Roth IRA conversion strategies took on momentum as a result of the 2017 tax laws that lowered income tax rates between the years 2018-2025. This new law allowed larger Roth IRA conversions in lower tax brackets. *Forbes* magazine featured our strategies, and we also had several posts in Forbes.com where I am a paid contributor.

As I previously mentioned, included in the Tax Cut and Jobs Act of 2017 was a temporary reduction of the income tax brackets. In 2017, the 25% tax bracket for married filing jointly taxpayers used to top out at $153,100. In 2019, the 24% tax bracket topped out at $321,450. For 2020 the top of the 24% bracket is $326,600. So, in the last chapter we talked about using the 24% tax bracket after death with the Schwartz 24% Optimizer. Now, we are talking about optimizing the 24% bracket during your lifetime.

These reduced tax rates are scheduled to revert to the old rates at the end of 2025. They also might go up with a change of administration. In addition, as previously mentioned, someone is going to have to pay for the 2.5 trillion-dollar bail out for CARES. After "running the numbers" more and more, we are finding ourselves recommending that many age 70+ or now age 72+ year-old clients (the difference is the new rules for when the RMD kicks in) continue executing Roth conversions even though they are already taking RMDs and receiving Social Security benefits. Though every taxpayer's situation is unique, it is an interesting idea to consider making Roth conversions in the 24% tax bracket when you know future RMDs will be taxed at higher tax rates once the current tax rates increase.

While on the topic of tax brackets for Roth IRA conversion purposes, please realize if you are married now you are likely filing as married-filing-jointly taxpayers. These rates are significantly lower than single tax rates. After the first spouse of the couple dies, the surviving spouse will likely have a similar income except that there will be one Social Security benefit instead of two. But the surviving spouse will be in a much higher tax bracket so Roth IRA conversions will not be as attractive as when you are both alive and married filing jointly.

Hopefully, you already have part of your retirement in Roth IRAs. I have been recommending "running the numbers" to determine the best strategies for years. Many times, the result of that analysis is to propose a series of Roth IRA conversions over a period of years. Most IRA owners should have a long-term Roth IRA conversion strategy integrated into their retirement and estate plan.

Finally, fair warning. One negative recent change to the Roth IRA conversion law is that you are no longer allowed to make a Roth IRA conversion and undo it (technically recharacterize the Roth IRA conversion). Under old law, you could make a Roth IRA conversion and if the underlying investment went down or you changed your mind, you could undo it or technically recharacterize the Roth IRA conversion. No longer. So, if you make a Roth IRA conversion and the market goes down and never recovers, you will likely be worse off than if you did nothing.

How the Market Impact of COVID-19 Makes Roth IRA Conversions More Attractive

As we go to press, the S&P 500 is down roughly 10% from its peak due to COVID-19. I would like to emphasize three great reasons why *now* is likely a great time to do a Roth IRA conversion.

1. Though I am not a market timer, history suggests that after a downturn, even if it takes years, there will be a significant recovery. So, if the market goes up after we make a Roth IRA conversion, we will, in effect, be getting a Roth IRA at bargain rates. Let's say I have an IRA invested in a low-cost index fund that was valued at $133,000 at its peak and today its value is $100,000. You make a Roth IRA conversion on the $100,000 and you pay tax on $100,000. The market rebounds and now your Roth IRA is worth $133,000. You just got a great bargain by paying tax on $100,000 and getting a $133,000 Roth IRA.

2. Most of our Roth IRA conversion analysis assumes that the federal income tax rate is going to stay steady for a few years at least. But the $2.5 trillion bailout casts a shadow over that assumption. Who is likely to pay for it? Not the poor. If history is any indication, not the billionaires. It will probably be some combination of you and your heirs, people with large IRAs and retirement plans and other high-income taxpayers. Between our current deficit and the new $2.5 trillion bailout, it isn't a huge leap to think tax rates are going up. In addition, we are already in a historically low tax environment. In 2017, a mar-

ried couple filing jointly with a taxable income of $326,600 was in the 33% tax bracket. Thanks to the Tax Cuts and Jobs Act of 2017, today that couple would be in the 24% tax bracket. If you make a Roth IRA conversion now and income tax rates go up in the future, you will have made a Roth IRA conversion at bargain rates. If you think tax rates will increase over the long run and specifically increase for you, then Roth IRA conversions can be a great idea.

3. Another area to consider is that if you are currently married, you are likely filing using the favorable married filing jointly income tax rates. The year after one of you dies, the survivor will likely be filing as a single taxpayer, and the income tax rates will be much higher. Other than the fact that the survivor will have only one Social Security benefit rather than two benefits, the income itself will likely be similar. Yes, there could be a disclaimer filed utilizing the Schwartz 24% Maximizer, but the point is that income tax rates will usually be higher.

4. Many advisors are recommending you rebalance your portfolio by putting more money in the market right now when it is low. I am not saying that is wrong, but it is certainly uncomfortable. If the market stays low for a long time, there might not be much of a short-term benefit with rebalancing. On the other hand, even if the market stays low, a Roth IRA conversion will likely be beneficial for you and your family. It is also a way of leveraging your money to lock in tax-free gains for you, your spouse and your family.

How the Market Impact of the Coronavirus Aid, Relief, and Economic Security Act (CARES Act) Creates Immediate Planning Opportunities

The $2.5 trillion dollar Coronavirus Aid, Relief, and Economic Security Act (CARES Act) temporarily suspends the RMD requirement from Traditional IRAs and retirement plans. If you are 71 or older, unless you need the money and depend on it for your cash flow, consider foregoing your RMD for 2020. That will help stem losses from having to take your RMD while the market is down. If you are receiving your RMDs through monthly automatic transfers from your IRA to your checking, you might want to stop that transfer.

With respect to Roth IRA conversions, not taking your RMD can make doing a Roth IRA conversion even more desirable because it might keep or put you in a favorable tax bracket by reducing your taxable income. If you were already planning on a Roth IRA conversion, perhaps this will give you an opportunity to convert an even larger amount.

Even more, for 2020 the CARES Act temporarily increases the federal income tax deduction for charitable contributions up to 100% of a taxpayer's AGI. For those very charitable donors already giving more than 60% of their income, a large donation, made directly to a charity, would result in a large charitable contribution deduction that if paired with a Roth IRA conversion could result in no or reduced federal income tax owed on the Roth IRA conversion.

Finally, consider how the confluence of these factors could make *now* the best time in history to make a Roth IRA conversion.

I posted an article on Forbes.com with information similar to that in this chapter, and it received 130,000 views in the first two days. I called the article *Now is the Best Time In History To Do a Roth IRA Conversion*. Please see **www.pay taxeslater.com** to access the original article.

Consider how the confluence of these factors could make now the best time in history to make a Roth IRA conversion.

Running the Numbers

One of the things we do for our clients is to "run the numbers" as part of a financial masterplan. As I mentioned earlier, "running the numbers" is our shorthand for a detailed analysis of a client's finances, financial decisions, and the tax implications under different scenarios. One of the purposes of running the numbers is to determine an ideal long-term Roth IRA conversion plan. Of course, Roth IRA conversions are only one aspect of running the numbers. We believe a well-integrated plan includes Social Security strategies, spending strategies, gifting strategies, estate planning, asset location, etc.

Unfortunately, many of our new clients don't start with an integrated retirement and estate plan; their "plan" is the result of a bunch of individual decisions that all made sense *at the time they were made*. For example, they may have picked an asset allocation for their 401(k) with the help of a benefits plan administrator or an advisor at work. Then, either on their own or with another advisor, they picked investments for their money outside of their retirement plan. Maybe they contributed to a Roth IRA or even made several Roth IRA conversions. Then, they saw an attorney and drafted a will. Then they saw an insurance guy and got some insurance.

In other words, what you have now is not likely part of an integrated plan taking everything into account, including money, desires, family situation, taxes, etc. What you have now is likely the result of a bunch of individual decisions, all of which seemed to make sense at the time they were made.

Even if you had a plan, that plan may need to be reconsidered in light of COVID-19 and CARES.

We prefer to have an integrated synergistic plan accounting for all of your assets, income, goals and dreams, family situation, etc. But, the basic premise of this chapter is that at some point in your life, a partial Roth IRA conversion, at a minimum, will likely be a great strategy for both you and your heirs. Even under the new law (accelerating the tax on your IRA at death and accelerating the distribution of the Inherited Roth IRA), making a series of Roth IRA conversions is likely to improve your and your spouse's financial position. It is also likely that it will significantly improve your children's financial situation after you and your spouse die.

In other words, what you have now is not likely part of an integrated plan taking everything into account, including money, desires, family situation, taxes, etc. What you have now is likely the result of a bunch of individual decisions, all of which seemed to make sense at the time they were made.

One of the reasons I describe "running the numbers" is because I don't believe that decisions about Roth IRA conversions should be a matter of opinion: "I like the idea of a Roth conversion, let's do it." There are too many factors to consider before someone should decide to go ahead with a conversion. And then, even if a Roth IRA conversion is appropriate, how much of a conversion should you do and when should you do it?

For example, if you convert too much in any one year, you might push yourself into a much higher tax bracket and, ultimately you and your family will be worse off than if you did nothing or if you made a smaller Roth IRA conversion. Some years it will not make sense to do a Roth IRA conversion.

I will be the first to admit that Roth IRA conversions are not perfect or even appropriate for everyone. But even with the uncertainties, I believe, with the help of an appropriate advisor, you can determine an optimal short and long-term Roth IRA conversion plan.

What I am getting at is that, although we have to deal with the uncertainty of future tax rates and the uncertainty of the market, I believe that there is an ideal Roth IRA conversion strategy in terms of when to convert and how much to convert each year. That plan can best be discovered by "running the numbers" which tests the outcomes for many different strategies. Of course, when we run the numbers Roth IRA conversions, are only one variable that we test, but that is the focus of this chapter.

After you have developed a long-term Roth IRA conversion plan, the plan should be updated every year to get the most out of what you've got. We have a lot of quantitative clients, often retired engineers, who attempt to do this by plotting variables in Excel spreadsheets. Sometimes they find a better solution than doing nothing. On the other hand, they aren't tax experts, and they often neglect to factor in critical considerations.

We have a huge advantage. We possess excellent software and, more importantly, highly skilled CPAs who know tax law inside out. Anticipating that the stretch IRA was going to be killed, they also have many years of experience "running the numbers" and developing masterplans to combat the death of the stretch IRA.

The other thing that is easier for us to calculate—in contrast to some of the do-it-yourselfers—are the long-term impacts of Roth IRA conversions, i.e., 20 to 50 or more years into the future. Yes, most of us will be gone in 50 years or maybe much less, but our children and/or grandchildren will still be here.

The changes to the Inherited IRA rules reduce the long-term benefits of Roth IRA conversions, because the beneficiary will no longer benefit from the lifetime stretch of the Inherited Roth IRA. (On the other hand, in most cases, inheriting a Roth IRA is much better for a beneficiary than inheriting a Traditional IRA because of the punitive income tax consequences.)

This is disappointing, but many gems remain for the IRA owner willing to learn when and how much of a Roth IRA conversion to make. Furthermore, Roth conversions will not be subject to required minimum distributions for either you or your spouse, and Roth IRA distributions are tax-free. A Roth IRA conversion will also reduce the amount of money held in a Traditional IRA that will be subject to accelerated income tax at your death. In all probability, it is an effective use of your time and/or money to develop a long-term Roth IRA conversion strategy. So, how do you decide to move forward?

Know the General Principles First, then Run the Numbers

Making changes to a retirement plan can be overwhelming and scary. You don't want to make a mistake, and it can seem safest just to stay put. I get it. I have a reputation for being a strong advocate for Roth IRA conversions for people of all ages. That reputation doesn't really reflect my beliefs. I believe this is a more accurate statement—*I am the owner of a firm that "runs the numbers" for our clients to make objective recommendations that often include making a series of Roth IRA conversions over several years.*

The advice and text that follow come from having overseen the "running of the numbers" (never to be confused with the "running of the bulls") literally thousands of times. In 1998, I wrote the first peer-reviewed article on Roth IRA conversions, which was published in the American Institute of CPAs journal, **The Tax Adviser.** I also wrote a dedicated bestselling book about Roth IRA conversions, which you can download for free at **https://paytaxeslater.com/books/**.

I have trained thousands of financial advisors, CPAs, and attorneys as well as consumers on the benefits of Roth IRA conversions. I continue to receive invitations to speak at some of the most prestigious estate planning conferences and feel well qualified to give this advice. (Forgive me if I seem a bit testy, but Roth IRA conversions can be so valuable in a retirement and estate plan that I hate to see my enthusiasm for effective planning summed up as the ideas of a fanatic.) I cannot overemphasize the potential benefits of an ideal long-term Roth IRA conversion plan.

Finally, if you want more third-party proof of the potential benefits of a Roth IRA conversion, consider this supporting information. Though the radio station is now off the air, for over five years, I had a financial radio talk show. I interviewed many of the top IRA experts in the country. We could quibble about who is on that list, but it includes the following well-known experts in the IRA and

---

I am the owner of a firm that "runs the numbers" for our clients to make objective recommendations that often include making a series of Roth IRA conversions over several years.

---

retirement plan professional community: Ed Slott, Natalie Choate, Bob Keebler, Martin Shenkman, Jane Bryant Quinn, Elaine Floyd, Barry Picker, and many more. All of them believed that at some point in the life of most IRA and retirement plan owners, a Roth IRA conversion of at least a portion of their IRA or retirement plan was an appropriate strategy.

The Secret: Quantifying the Benefit of Roth IRA Conversions Using the Concept of Purchasing Power

The following couple of paragraphs involve a critical concept that I have literally taught to tens of thousands of financial professionals, CPAs, attorneys, and IRA and retirement plan owners. I call it "the secret." Audiences often see IRAs and Roth IRAs in a different light after learning "the secret." It is a critical concept. Even if you don't have any interest in Roth IRA conversions, it will be well worth the effort to try to understand "the secret."

Although you may have to read these paragraphs a second time, the rewards for understanding the secret could make a significant difference in your life. CPAs will likely understand it reading it the first time. Most other readers will understand "the secret" either after the first or maybe the second time reading about it. Attorneys will take about three times reading it or they might never get it. You think I am kidding, but my general workshop attendees, who to be fair are pretty smart, usually pick up on this concept faster than my attorney audiences.

The Secret

In short, the secret is to start thinking in terms of "purchasing power" *vs.* "total dollars." For example, if I have $1 million in my IRA, and you have $900,000 in an after-tax account, using a traditional definition of money, I have more money than you because I have a million dollars and you only have $900,000.

But what if we both want to make a large purchase? I have to cash in my IRA and pay the taxes. Let's assume a flat income tax rate of 24%. I know that isn't realistic, but this is to demonstrate a concept. After taxes, I'd end up with $760,000 in cash. (This ignores the tax on the money needed to pay the tax, but I want to keep this simple.) Unless there are capital gains that need to be considered, when you cash out your $900,000, there will be no taxes. That means you can purchase more goods and services with your $900,000 after-tax dollars than I can with my $1,000,000 IRA. You have more purchasing power than I have. I submit that a better measure of wealth is purchasing power, as opposed to "whoever has the most money wins."

For the purposes of measuring wealth, can we use the concept of purchasing power rather than total dollars? May I safely assume you would rather have $900,000 in after-tax funds than a $1,000,000 IRA?

Now Let's Look at Roth Conversions in Terms of Purchasing Power

Let's do another head to head, apples to apples comparison. Both of us have $100,000 in our IRAs and $24,000 outside of our IRAs. I will assume a flat income tax rate of 24% as I did previously. I don't make a Roth IRA conversion. Measured in total dollars, I have $124,000. But, if I think of that amount in "purchasing power," I have $100,000 *($124,000 IRA – $24,000 tax that will be due when I cash the IRA in = $100,000).*

Now starting out with the same $100,000 in your IRA and $24,000 outside your IRA, you make a Roth IRA conversion of your entire IRA. Because you converted your IRA (which you hadn't yet paid taxes on) to the Roth IRA, you will have to fork over $24,000 of after-tax dollars to Uncle Sam ($100,000 times 24% tax rate). But, after the conversion, you will have a $100,000 Roth IRA. You will also have $100,000 measured in both total dollars and purchasing power because there will be no tax due when you cash in your Roth IRA.

The table below shows that, when measured in terms of purchasing power and using simple assumptions, the breakeven point on Roth IRA conversions is Day 1, regardless of your age.

Roth IRA Value after Conversion		$ 100,000
Traditional IRA	$ 100,000	
Other Non-IRA Funds*	24,000	0
Total Dollar Value of Accounts	$ 124,000	$ 100,000
Less Taxes Paid on IRA (if distributed)	(24,000)	0
Purchasing Power	$ 100,000	$ 100,000

* Non-IRA Funds of $24,000 Used to Pay Tax On Conversion

Using the Non-IRA Funds of $24,000 to Pay the Tax on the Roth IRA Conversion

Let's look at this issue another way, but one that will lead to the same conclusion. If you were a farmer, would you rather deduct the cost of the seed but be required to pay tax on the harvest, or forego the deduction on the seed but reap the harvest tax-free? A Roth IRA conversion is like paying tax on the seed, or in this case, paying tax on the amount of your Traditional IRA that you want to convert. After you pay the tax, you plant the seed (open your new Roth IRA account with the money you have converted), and over many years, you watch it grow. Then when you or your heirs harvest the crop (the amount you converted plus all of the growth) the entire harvest is income-tax free. You pay taxes once and never again.

Roth IRA Conversions are Good for You During Your Lifetime

If you're already retired, is the tax-free advantage of the Roth conversion great enough to write a big check to Uncle Sam before you have to, let alone deal with all the paperwork? Have a look at Graph 6.1 at the top of page 94, which shows the outcome if you make seven Roth IRA conversions of $100,000 per year from the time you are 65 until you reach 72, compared to no Roth IRA conversions. Again, we measure in purchasing power, not total dollars.

It is hard to see but this shows that the IRA owner (that is you, not your kids) are better off by $124,399 if you make seven $100,000 Roth conversions starting as late as age 65 and assuming you survive until age 90. This assumes a 7% rate of return. *Please note if you make a Roth IRA conversion while the market is down due to COVID-19 and the market goes back up and tax rates increase, the value of the Roth IRA conversion will be significantly higher.*

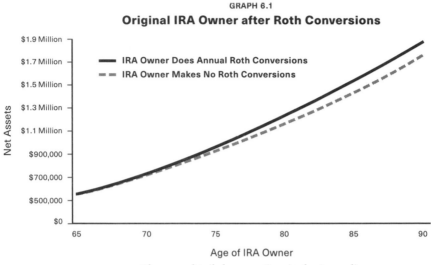

GRAPH 6.1
Original IRA Owner after Roth Conversions

Please see detailed assumptions in the Appendix.

This graph measures the accounts in terms of their relative purchasing power, which is the only way I can compare the value of an IRA to that of an after-tax account. Depending on your individual situation, it is likely that you will benefit during your lifetime by making a Roth conversion—or more likely, a series of smaller Roth IRA conversions. And the longer you and your spouse live, the more that benefit grows.

We analyzed the benefits for you and your spouse optimizing Roth IRA conversions and Social Security in Chapter 14 on page 137. If you wanted to learn more about why Roth IRA conversions are so good for you, in addition to being great for your heirs, please see our book, *The Roth Revolution* which you can download for free by going to **https://paytaxeslater.com/books/** or buy a hard copy or digital version on Amazon. Please note that while that book was written before the SECURE Act, virtually all the concepts remain the same, and it can still be a valuable resource. We also have a specialized video on Roth IRA conversions both before and after the SECURE Act. Please see the back of the book for video offers.

Roth IRA Conversions are Definitely Good for Your Heirs

So let's continue with the example above. Let's assume you start making Roth IRA conversions of $100,000/year at age 65 and continue until age 72. You die at age 85. Then you leave your estate to your 46-year-old child. Let's also assume

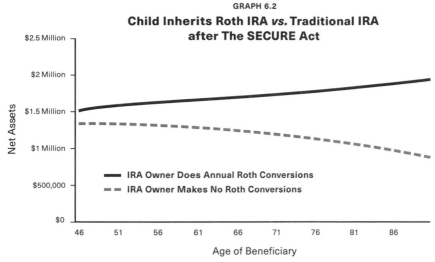

GRAPH 6.2
Child Inherits Roth IRA *vs.* Traditional IRA after The SECURE Act

Please see detailed assumptions in the Appendix.

you did not do any of the special planning regarding disclaimers covered in Chapter 5. You name your only child as the beneficiary of the Roth IRA. Your child now owns a special asset called an Inherited Roth IRA. Under the SECURE Act the entire Inherited Roth IRA account will have to be disbursed within 10 years of your death.

Losing the long-term tax-free growth on the Roth IRA over his or her lifetime will be costly to your child, but the Inherited Roth IRA is still more advantageous than the Inherited Traditional IRA.

Graph 6.2 above projects the differences between doing the seven $100,000 Roth IRA conversions versus doing nothing. This chart, however, shows the difference for your children, not for you. Though we have more details for this chart in the Appendix, the most important detail that you will find in the Appendix is that this chart takes into consideration the taxes you had to pay to make the Roth IRA conversion before you died.

Compare the dotted line (the Inherited Traditional IRA) to the dashed line (the Inherited Roth IRA). Even though both of these IRAs are stretched for only 10 years, inheriting the Roth (the dashed line) gives your child an additional $400,000 over the course of his lifetime. *Please note that if you make a Roth IRA conversion while the market is down due to COVID-19 and the market goes back up and tax rates increase, the value of the Roth IRA conversion to you and your children will be significantly higher.*

Are you thinking that you might want to make a Roth conversion? We recommend working with a firm that has expertise in "running the numbers" and that can make objective recommendations. It might be possible for an individual to "run their own numbers." We have a lot of engineers as clients and some engineers would rather have a root canal than pay an advisor. Often, they don't come up with the right conclusion, and I don't have enough space to list all the mistakes they make. But the mistakes are significant and would lead them to far from optimal results. That said, they may come up with a better conclusion than doing nothing.

Please be wary of the calculators on the internet. Most of the ones I have seen don't consider the concept of purchasing power and lead to the wrong conclusion. If you measure in total dollars instead of purchasing power, you will often conclude Roth IRA conversions are good for young IRA owners, but not good for older individuals. A young person will likely have a long enough investment horizon that they will make up for the fact that they had to write a check to the IRS in order to make their Roth IRA conversion. Seniors, on the other hand, will have a reduced time horizon and they might not make up for the money they had to pay in taxes in order to make a Roth IRA conversion. But, in both of those examples, we are measuring in total dollars instead of purchasing power which is the more appropriate measuring tool. When you take purchasing power into account, Roth IRA conversions are often advantageous for seniors as the analysis above suggests.

Running the numbers taking multiple variables into account is a fairly complicated calculation that has to take timing, taxes, and Social Security into account. (I know that is a self-serving recommendation because there are so few firms that can thoroughly run the numbers and come up with the right answer—but we pride ourselves on our skill set.)

We also make it our practice to have the client in the room, either in person or on Zoom or Skype, when we run their numbers. That way, the client can see how we arrive at our recommendations, and the client can discriminate among the assumptions and pick ones that best reflect his or her circumstances. In practice, when we run the numbers, Roth IRA conversions are only one of many factors that we compare. For example, we often also compare different Social Security strategies, different gifting strategies, different spending strategies, and lifestyle issues like buying or renting a second home in a warmer climate. We also often work backwards to determine how much money a client can safely spend. Evaluating the merits of Roth IRA conversions, though critical, is only one variable when we run the numbers. We are looking to develop a long-term financial masterplan for our clients.

You might assume that in today's world, there would be killer software where all you need to do is enter a few numbers, and *Poof!* the ideal Roth IRA conversion recommendation pops out. That isn't even close. Though we use the finest software we know, running the numbers is much more hands-on than you would imagine, and the skill of the person running the numbers is more important than the quality of the software they are using. Believe it or not, in addition to a variety of excellent software now on the market, in certain applications, we still use an Excel template that we developed years ago because we haven't found anything better. Other times the person running the numbers is using an Excel spreadsheet because no software that we know can adequately handle certain situations, and we have to make "manual" calculations.

It is also prudent to test the number you arrive at by actually preparing a mock tax return showing the impact that alternative courses of action may have. So, as an example, after arriving at a conclusion for the amount and the timing of a Roth IRA conversion, we will test that amount using all the facts and figures of a client's actual tax return in a mock tax return with the Roth IRA conversion amount included.

Even for veteran number crunchers, there are often surprises in this last step that cause us to change our recommendations, i.e., such as accidentally increasing the client's premium on Medicare Part B. More often than not, we have to go back to test different conversion amounts in order to find the optimal result. If you are curious about whether a Roth IRA conversion is beneficial for you and your family, here are some points to consider.

First, you can minimize the sticker shock as well as stay in a lower tax bracket if you make a series of small conversions over several years, rather than converting one large lump sum. One overly simplistic, though useful idea would be to convert, each year, only enough to bring you to the top of your existing tax bracket, or maybe moving into the next bracket if it made good long-term sense. For example, we sometimes recommend a 22% taxpayer make a large enough Roth IRA conversion to take them to the 24% bracket.

Second, you might have a window of opportunity that will result in a lower tax bill. If you stop working before age 72 (the new age to begin taking your RMDs, and one of the few good things about the SECURE Act—we will cover that later), you will have a number of years when your taxable income will be

One overly simplistic, though useful idea would be to convert, each year, only enough to bring you to the top of your existing tax bracket.

lower by comparison to when you will be required to take minimum distributions from your IRA. Delaying your Social Security benefits until age 70 also widens the window of opportunity and allows you to convert more money to a Roth IRA while still staying in a lower tax bracket.

Qualified charitable deductions (QCDs) and Roth IRA conversions are sometimes like peas and carrots. The reduced income from the QCD allows a bigger Roth IRA conversion at a lower tax rate.

If you can plan ahead, sometimes you can manipulate your income during retirement to make sure that the taxes that you pay on a Roth conversion are as low as possible. Please note we make similar calculations with regard to optimizing your Social Security strategy. Optimizing Social Security and Roth IRA conversions are often a synergistic calculation. For more about the various Social Security strategies, please download for free our bestselling Social Security book, *The $214,000 Mistake, How to Double Your Social Security & Maximize Your IRAs* by going to **https://paytaxeslater.com/books/**.

Finally, consider that tax rates will likely increase in the future and the value of paying taxes now at lower rates and making tax-free withdrawals at a later date will be even more favorable than all the analysis in this chapter indicates.

There are so many variables to consider in making Roth IRA conversions for retirement and estate planning purposes. It has been our longstanding practice when we run the numbers to determine the best long-term strategy for when and how much to convert to a Roth IRA. And while the advantages to your heirs can be impressive, our primary focus is on the advantages a conversion confers on our client. On the other hand, we ask what income tax bracket your children are in which is relevant for our calculations. We usually run our calculations through a reasonable projection for the life of your child or children.

It is also possible that after running the numbers, it becomes clear that you are not a suitable candidate for a Roth IRA conversion. One group of people it might not be beneficial for are taxpayers who have no money to pay the income tax on the conversion except by invading their IRA. Then, the math shows the Roth IRA conversion is a breakeven or maybe a little better and maybe better for your heirs, but not enough that we often recommend writing a check from your IRA to pay the taxes on the Roth conversion. Another example of someone who might not benefit from a Roth IRA conversion is someone who is leaving all their money to a charity.

There are certainly IRA owners who would not benefit from a Roth conversion. That said, we find that most of the IRA owners we see will benefit from developing and implementing a Roth IRA conversion strategy. Determining your best plan is a great use of your time, and if you find the right advisor to help you, a great use of your money.

Also, please go into the process of determining how much and when to convert to a Roth IRA with an open mind. One client was unhappy when the results of our projections of our best recommendations still left him with a significant IRA at the end of his lifetime. He was hoping for a plan that would have converted everything to a Roth. In his case, that would have pushed him into too high an income tax bracket, and both he and his family would have been worse off if we blindly followed his wishes of gradually converting everything to a Roth before he died. Remember, in God we trust, all others bring data.

Of course, this short chapter can't tell you everything you need to know about Roth IRA conversions, which is why I am giving you a link to a free download of my book, ***The Roth Revolution, Pay Taxes Once and Never Again*** at **https:// paytaxeslater.com/books/**.

KEY IDEAS *(Part 1)*

- Most IRA owners should be proactive about at least considering and more likely developing a long-term Roth IRA conversion strategy.

- The convergence of the market being low due to COVID-19 and tax rates being low could and no RMD in 2020 make this the perfect time for many IRA owners to begin a series of Roth IRA conversions.

- To appreciate Roth IRA conversions, you have to understand the idea of purchasing power *vs.* total dollars.

- The current low tax brackets add incentive to explore Roth IRA conversions.

KEY IDEAS *(Part 2)*

- An integrated retirement and estate plan that takes your assets, income, goals and dreams, family situation, etc. into account is decidedly advantageous.

- Roth IRA conversions are not for everyone, but the only way to really assess the situation is to "run the numbers."

- Your heirs will benefit more from inheriting Roth IRAs than traditional IRAs.

- Running the numbers can result in much better decisions than winging it.

Navigate Retirement and Estate Planning with Your Own Personalized "Financial Masterplan"

Your current financial situation is almost certainly the result of many individual decisions made at separate times, each of which seemed like a good idea at the time. For example:

- At work, your benefits administrator may have advised you on the allocation of assets in your retirement plan.

- Later, you may have had an advisor or even a friend give you advice or a tip on outside investments.

- At some point, you saw an attorney who did a will and trust for you.

- You also saw a life insurance agent and purchased a term life insurance policy.

- And maybe, either on your own or with the advice of a CPA, you may have done some Roth IRA conversions.

At **Lange Financial Group**, we start the *Masterplan* process by first looking at your entire financial and family picture as it is today, no matter how it got to where it is now.

Then, we come up with a plan that touches on all of the areas mentioned above and more. The left hand always knows what the right hand is doing. So, instead of a disorganized and scattered approach, every component of your wealth is integrated into a clear, strategic Financial Masterplan.

The unified *Financial Masterplan* we create for you takes *all* of your financial attributes into consideration, including:

- The amount of money you can safely spend.
- Net worth.
- Roth IRA conversions.
- Social Security options.
- Gifting strategies.
- Insurance.
- Estate planning.

We look at your unique issues, and then run your numbers to produce a personalized *Financial Masterplan*. Result: we get your financial house in order, ensuring that you and your family are financially secure and well taken care of.

Please note that *Lange Financial Masterplans* are often in heavy demand. And new clients are accepted on a first come, first serve basis.

Not long ago, two of my CPAs asked me to stop offering these *Masterplan* running the numbers engagements because they were putting in extremely long hours and working nights and weekends to get all the work done.

My two CPAs finally caught up with their backlog, so we are once again accepting more "running the numbers" engagements—but there really are a limited number we can take on. Again, at least at this point, these meetings are virtual on Zoom.

If you are interested, we urge you to phone us now toll-free at **1-800-387-1129**. The charge is usually $7,500, but it can be more if there are unusual circumstances or the estate is larger than $10 million.

The free Zoom or phone conversation at this point would be with me until I am overwhelmed and then it would be with one of the two people who would actually do the work. On the other hand, if I get on the phone, I dictate all the strategies that that I can think of which should be tested when we finally do "run the numbers." If I don't think you would benefit from the service, I will tell you that too. One purpose of the call is to determine if you and your situation would be the right fit and could derive huge benefits from this service. There is no cost for the call. And no obligation of any kind.

7

Tax-Loss Harvesting

Tax-loss harvesting is an important tax planning strategy that I could not leave out. We write about tax-loss harvesting every year in our year-end tax planning letter, but a better practice is to do tax-loss harvesting throughout the year, particularly after a drop in the market. All of the money management firms that we work with have been extremely busy with tax-loss harvesting since the outbreak of COVID-19.

Basically, to tax-loss harvest, you sell a stock or a fund that is currently at a lower share price than when you bought it. To properly execute this strategy, you can't just select a stock that is down for the year and sell your shares; this is about selling a stock that is currently trading for less than the price you paid for your shares.

Most readers with money outside their IRAs and retirement plans have significant appreciation in those investments. If some of those highly appreciated investments are now under water, at a break-even point, or at a price that would only incur a small capital gain, selling them while they are down may be a great strategy. Of course, this only works in a taxable account, not an IRA or retirement plan.

Adam Yofan of Buckingham Strategic Wealth offers the following simple example on the next page.

	Harvest	Do Nothing
January 1, 2020 Value	$ 100	$ 100
Value at Time of Sale	$ 70	$ 70
Harvest-Sell	**$ 70**	
December 31, 2020 Value		
(Assume market goes back to January 1, 2020 level)	$ 100	$ 100
Tax Deduction or Loss to be Utilized	$ 30	$ 0
Tax Saved 27% (24% Fed. + 3% PA)	$ 8	$ 0
Portfolio + Tax Saved	$ 108	$ 100

Of course, tax-loss harvesting could lead to permanent tax decreases and/or greater tax deferral. In either case, it will save you money.

There is an important limitation. You can't sell a stock, claim the loss, and buy it back the next day. The rule with a stock or fund sold for a tax-loss is that you have to wait 30 days before you can buy back the same security in a taxable account. This is known as the wash rule. But you can probably get around that rule by buying something similar to the security you just sold for a loss.

You can use an unlimited amount of capital losses to offset capital gains. For those higher income taxpayers, lowering current year investment income by loss harvesting will generate even greater savings. These taxpayers can potentially lower the net investment income tax (the additional 3.8% tax) assessed on net investment income above certain levels.

This topic deserves a lot more attention, but it is beyond the scope of this book.

8

Charitable Remainder Trusts Deserve a Serious Second Look After the SECURE Act

Even if Your Primary Goal is Protecting Your Family

"Wealth is not new. Neither is charity. But the idea of using private wealth imaginatively, constructively, and systematically to attack the fundamental problems of mankind is new."

— John Gardner

The Big Picture with Charitable Remainder Trusts

Before we get immersed in the details, the big picture is that there are many situations where your children would get more money and a steadier income if you named a charitable remainder trust as the beneficiary of your IRA than if you named your children directly. If you have a million dollars or more in your IRA, even if you aren't very charitable, you should at least consider naming a charitable remainder trust as the beneficiary of your IRA. One of the goals of this book is to further my initiative to help direct a billion dollars to charity while securing more money and a long-lasting legacy for the children of IRA owners.

What is a Charitable Remainder Trust?

First of all, when I say a charitable remainder trust, what am I talking about?

In this context, I am talking about naming a charitable remainder trust as the beneficiary of your IRA or retirement plan. Of course, if you are married, you would name your surviving spouse as the primary beneficiary. This chapter compares naming your children as the contingent beneficiaries after your spouse (or your children as primary beneficiaries if you don't have a spouse) *vs.* naming a charitable remainder trust with your children as the income beneficiaries.

To oversimplify, the trust would provide your beneficiary (let's assume your child) with a distribution that has some, but not a complete correlation to the income of the trust, and then at the child's death the amount remaining in the trust would go to the charity of your or even your child's choice. Actuarially, the charitable remainder trust must be set up in a way that the charity receives at least 10% of the present value of the bequest at the date of death; but that leaves 90% for your children. When you take into account the enormous tax benefits of the charitable remainder unitrust, a type of trust we favor called a CRUT and the draconian tax treatment of leaving your IRA to your children directly, your children often get more value, sometimes by hundreds of thousands of dollars, than if you just outright leave the IRA to them.

The big picture is that there are many situations where your children would get more money and a steadier income if you named a charitable remainder trust as the beneficiary of your IRA than if you named your children directly.

Is a charitable remainder trust an appropriate solution or even partial solution to respond to the SECURE Act? For many families, absolutely. For other families, definitely not. For others it becomes a matter of preference and values. We will present the arguments in favor of and against CRTs, and the math of charitable trusts as beneficiaries of IRAs versus naming your children directly as beneficiaries of your IRA.

Below we present the very favorable math of the charitable trust for your family. Having charity in your heart is a major bonus. If you like the idea of maintaining a significant amount of money in the tax deferred environment and having your beneficiary get regular distributions for the rest of his or her life, especially if it results in more money for your children, then charitable remainder trusts should at least be considered.

The charitable trust can to some extent be treated as a stretch IRA.

To get the best results, leaving your IRA to someone other than your spouse requires strategic planning. Let's go back to exempt beneficiaries.

In addition to your spouse and other classes of exceptions, charities and charitable trusts are also exempt from the 10-year tax acceleration rule. To use this exemption to the 10-year tax acceleration rule, you could establish a Charitable Remainder Unitrust (CRUT), or Charitable Remainder Annuity Trust (CRAT) and name it as the beneficiary of your IRA (after your spouse, if appropriate).

So, to be clear, this trust is a testamentary trust meaning that it isn't funded before you and your spouse die. While you are alive, there is no tax return, no money goes into it, and other than some paper sitting in a fireproof drawer, it doesn't exist. It is totally revocable meaning you can change it as long as you and/or your spouse are alive. But, after you and your spouse die, if you name it as the beneficiary of your IRA or retirement plan, it comes to life.

Here's how a CRUT (or a CRAT with minor differences) works at the basic level. When you die or when both you and your spouse are dead, what remains, (a portion is also an option, but what remains in the IRA would be taxed on withdrawal) of your IRA could be transferred to a CRUT and the IRA can then be liquidated without paying taxes.

The conventional approach would be to leave your IRA directly to your children and/or grandchildren and all of it will be taxed in 10 years. With a CRUT, your children won't get a lump sum of money when you die—but they also will not face a big tax bill immediately after you die or as big a tax bill even 10 years after you die. They would receive a regular "income" from the CRUT for the rest of their lives. The distribution from the CRUT to your child would be treated as ordinary income until the amount of the initial IRA plus any interest and dividends earned in the CRUT has been paid to your child. After the ordinary income has been distributed, then capital gains would be distributed from the CRUT to your child and that distribution would receive the more favorable capital gains rates. Finally, when your children die, whatever is left in the CRUT goes to the charity of your or their choice.

Although you probably have some charity in your heart, you would most likely rather see your children get the bulk of your money rather than your favorite charity. Me too. The reason that this is an idea worth considering is that the money that goes into the CRUT—in this case, your IRA—isn't subject to the new rules governing after-death IRA distributions.

A CRUT, since it is an exempt beneficiary, can mimic the benefits of the stretch IRA by paying out the IRA income over a period of more than ten years and providing your heirs with a steady income over their entire lifetimes. Distributions from a CRUT can be stretched and taxed over your child's life (if you have no spouse) or after the deaths of you and your spouse. We like to look at everyone's unique situation and we like to do the math. The IRA must be large enough to make the CRUT a reasonable option.

Disadvantages of a CRUT

- Steve Kohman, our veteran CPA number-cruncher, points out that the biggest disadvantage of the CRUT is that the child does not have access to more of the inheritance if more money is needed at a particular point in the child's lifetime. He is right. On the other hand, if you have after-tax or Roth dollars that you are leaving to a child directly, this will reduce this disadvantage.

- You need to have an attorney draft the CRUT.

- You need to name a trustee.

- You can expect to pay an additional $500 to $2,000 (or sometimes more) every year for the remainder of the beneficiary's life, to maintain the trust from a legal and tax compliance standpoint. You not only need to file a special CRUT tax return, but you also must file a K-1 with the beneficiary which complicates his return. The additional complication and aggravation of drafting and, more importantly, maintaining the charitable trust for the life of your child or children should not be underestimated.

- The trustee of the CRUT is required to report the income that the beneficiary receives to the IRS and must send to each beneficiary a form called a K-1 which complicates the beneficiary's own tax return. If your beneficiary lives for 20 years, it's not unrealistic to think that the fees required to maintain the trust could exceed $20,000 or even $40,000.

- Ultimately you could be creating significant complications for less tax savings than you would have realized if you had just left the money to your child instead of the CRUT.

- If you leave your IRA to a CRUT, it could potentially hurt your family. If the income beneficiary of the trust (most likely, your child) dies prematurely, the remaining balance will go to the named charity and not to your grandchild as it would if you just left the IRA to your child. So, there is a very real risk with a CRUT, and it would likely not be an appropriate choice if your beneficiary has a reduced life expectancy.

Advantages of a CRUT

- Shirl Trefelner, another one of our number crunching CPAs, who actually did the quantitative analysis on CRUTS for this book sees it a little differently. She says "Look at the numbers. Including a CRUT as part of your estate plan may make an enormous difference for the long-term security of your child or children and it may be the best way to maximize the number of dollars your child receives. If you have charity in your heart as well as the desire to protect your family, it may be a wonderful thing."

Let's compare leaving your million-dollar IRA to a CRUT versus leaving it to your child. What is the best distribution option for the $1 million dollars if you leave the IRA to your child and the child will have to pay income taxes on the entire million (plus growth) within 10 years of your death? Though we could do some post-mortem planning, it will be extremely difficult to protect that distribution from very high tax rates that are projected to get even higher in the future.

The Essence of the Simple Math

To oversimplify, the income tax on the $1 million Inherited IRA could be $400,000, leaving your child with net proceeds after taxes of $600,000 plus appreciation. On the other hand, the CRUT pays no income taxes when you die. So, the income that your child will receive is based on $1 million, not $600,000. Let's assume for the moment you don't care about charity. Would you rather have your daughter get $600,000 outright or the income on $1,000,000? The answer will depend on a number of variables, but the most important variable is how long will your daughter live? If she survives you by one year and gets income for a year and then dies and the remainder of the trust goes to charity, that would be a bad deal for the family.

An Example by the Numbers of CRUT *vs.* Naming Your Child Outright

What I will show below is that your child will likely get more money over their lifetime as the beneficiary of a CRUT than if she receives your $1 million IRA outright.

Let's look at an example. Suppose Alice creates a CRUT that names her daughter, Roberta, as the income beneficiary, and her favorite charity (or charities) as the remainder beneficiary.

Roberta won't inherit the IRA directly, but she will receive a nice check from the CRUT on a regular basis for her entire life. The amount that she would receive is described in the section below titled Nitty Gritty Details of the CRUTs and CRATs.

So, which inheritance will benefit Roberta the most—the money outright subject to accelerated taxes or the income from the CRUT? The answer is it depends on what interest rates you assume but, perhaps more importantly, it depends on how long Roberta lives.

Given certain reasonable assumptions, including significant spending, Roberta would have $465,175 left at age 81 if her mom, Alice, left her IRA to a CRUT with Roberta as the income beneficiary. In addition, with the CRUT, if Roberta died at 81, Alice's favorite charity would receive $452,211 at Roberta's death. If Roberta lives past age 81, she will continue to receive an income and the charity would likely end up getting less money.

If Alice had left Roberta the IRA outright, given all the same assumptions, Roberta would have no money at age 81 and the charity would get no money.

Please don't overlook the implications of this calculation. Given reasonable assumptions, including significant annual spending, your child could have $465,175 at age 81 if you name your million-dollar IRA to a CRUT as the beneficiary of your IRA. Your favorite charity would get $452,211. Given those same assumptions, if you named your child outright as the beneficiary of your IRA, at

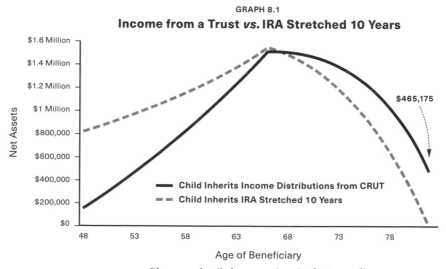

GRAPH 8.1
Income from a Trust *vs.* IRA Stretched 10 Years

Please see detailed assumptions in the Appendix.

Please don't overlook the implications of this calculation. Given reasonable assumptions, including significant annual spending, your child could have $465,175 at age 81 if you name your million-dollar IRA to a CRUT as the beneficiary of your IRA. Your favorite charity would get $452,211. Given those same assumptions, if you named your child outright as the beneficiary of your IRA, at age 81 your child would be broke and your charity would get nothing. The big loser with the CRUT is the IRS.

age 81 your child would be broke and your charity would get nothing. The big loser with the CRUT is the IRS.

Roberta only has to live past the age of 67 to receive more money from the CRUT as compared to inheriting the $1 million IRA stretched over ten years. (The breakeven point may change depending on your circumstances, what assumptions you use, the Section 7520 rate when the CRUT is created and how old your beneficiary is at your death.) The other advantage of the CRUT is that she will have all the protections of a trust including protection from creditors, protection from herself, and in some cases, financial protection from her husband—should she divorce or the marriage survives and her husband has different ideas on how she should spend her money.

As mentioned earlier, a legitimate objection to the CRUT is that if the income beneficiary dies young, his or her immediate family will get less money because after the death of the beneficiary, rather than the balance going to the grandchildren, it will go to the charity. That is true. An easy and inexpensive solution to that objection is to purchase term life insurance on the income beneficiary. If the income beneficiary dies prematurely, his or her children, i.e., your grandchildren, would be provided for by the insurance. Without going into that scenario at length, suffice it to say we ran the numbers and found the insurance solution strong enough to overcome or at least lessen the "leaving out the grandchildren in the event your child dies early" objection to doing a CRUT.

Finally, there is another interesting benefit that is hard to quantify. One of the provisions of the charitable remainder trusts is that it allows either you or the beneficiary to choose the charity. Assuming you trust the judgment of your child who would be the lifetime income beneficiary, giving your child the ability to choose the end beneficiary has the advantage of getting your child or children interested in philanthropy earlier in their lifetime. Hopefully, the child would begin a research project on a variety of charities and not just look at the stated purpose of the charity, but also how much money was effectively spent on charitable works and how much was spent on administration and fundraising.

Then, at that point they might also become involved in the charity, maybe to the point of directing the funds to certain purposes within the charity. For example, you or your child may prefer that a charitable contribution to a university be used to fund scholarships rather than a new building, etc.

Even if you aren't charitable, the potential benefits of the CRUT should certainly be considered if you like the idea of your child getting a regular income for the rest of their lives. If you are even a little bit charitable, the CRUT makes a lot of sense for a lot of IRA and retirement plan owners.

Your children can then be named as the income beneficiaries of the CRUT. You could also name your spouse as the primary beneficiary and the CRUT as the contingent beneficiary. If your spouse doesn't need the money, she can disclaim all or part of it to the CRUT.

The amount that the income beneficiaries receive from the CRUT will be based on their own life expectancies, and at their deaths, the remainder will go to a charity that either you or the beneficiaries designate.

Also, though I already mentioned it, the costs and aggravation of setting up and maintaining the trust are not inconsequential and need to be put into perspective.

Though we don't have a hard and fast number, our rule of thumb is that if the value of the Inherited IRA is much less than $1,000,000 then the costs and aggravation of the trust may well exceed its value. In this case, the trust would be funded with $1,000,000 which meets our "Is the amount going to the CRUT large enough to be worth the aggravation of setting up and maintaining a CRUT?" rule of thumb.

For IRA owners who like some of the charitable aspects of a CRUT and the forced gradual distribution of the IRA proceeds, it might be reasonable to consider doing a CRUT with significantly less than a $1,000,000 balance.

There are also some extremely interesting methods of combining life insurance planning with CRUTS and CRATs. That is beyond the scope of this book, but the reader should be aware that opportunities not presented here also exist.

Nitty Gritty Details of the CRUTs and CRATs

To spare big picture readers some grief, I have simplified this chapter, but feel honor bound to go into some details for those who are interested.

I will discuss two types of charitable remainder trusts as the beneficiary of an IRA or retirement plan:

1. Charitable Remainder Annuity Trusts (CRATs)
2. Charitable Remainder Unitrusts (CRUTs)

The CRAT pays a fixed income stream to the beneficiary from the time of death of the IRA owner until the death of the "income" beneficiary. The CRUT pays a fixed percentage to the beneficiary rather than a fixed amount.

In a CRAT, if the IRA were valued at $1,000,000 and the payout percentage was 6%, the distribution to the income beneficiary would be a flat $60,000 per year.

For a CRUT, it is a trickier calculation, but often results in a higher distribution for your child. I have been using the term "income," but that really isn't accurate. When determining the payout rate, you must project that what is left at the death of the income beneficiary will, on an actuarial basis, be at least 10% of the amount originally transferred to the charitable trust. To get even more technical, an individual can establish a CRUT to maximize the lifetime payout to the individual beneficiary provided that the payout does not exceed an amount that would cause an amount less than 10% of the present value of the amount used to fund the trust to be paid to charity.

For example, suppose you die with a CRUT as the beneficiary of your IRA and your beneficiary is currently 45 years old. As we go to press, the current Section 7520 rate is 2.0% and it is practically at an historic low.

Even with the currently low Section 7520 rates, the Trustee can still make a maximum permitted annual distribution to the beneficiary of 8.1% of the annual value of the CRUT. The Section 7520 interest rate is used to calculate what percentage of the trust can be distributed to your beneficiary. The higher the 7520 rate and the higher the age of the beneficiary, the higher the percentage of the trust that can be distributed to the beneficiary.

The point of all this is that if the 7520 rate goes up, as it likely will, and if your child is older than age 45 and your child keeps aging which, assuming he survives, is a certainty, the amount going to your family could be even more favorable than indicated above. Of course, if the market takes a downturn, as we are seeing in the spring of 2020, there is always the possibility that income distributions will decrease.

You also have the choice of distributing the CRUT over a fixed number of years. Your beneficiary's life expectancy might be 80, but you think she will only need distributions for the next 20 years. Using the same Section 7520 rate of 2% and choosing a fixed 20-year payout, the annual distribution would be 10.9% of the account balance. This provides a higher annual income for your beneficiary and still calculates the 10% distribution to charity at the end of the 20-year income payout. I don't recommend making the distribution period too short, simply because you defeat the purpose of keeping the annual distributions low in our effort to minimize the tax consequence for your beneficiary.

We recently drafted a CRUT for the benefit of a child who has a significantly reduced life expectancy. If we left the IRA to the child outright, it would have all been taxed in ten years after the IRA owner's death. If we used a CRUT for the life of the child, the income would not have been sufficient for the child's needs. Using the reduced life expectancy was the perfect solution for that child.

While IRA owners who want the most for their children and the least for their charity want the highest payout rate for the trust, there is also a limitation on the lower interest range. The rules for CRUTs include an annual minimum payout rate of 5%. This means that any beneficiary 28 or younger will get the same 5% annual payout. The younger beneficiary would just get those payments for a longer period of time.

Finally, one more technical point. If you name a CRAT or a CRUT as the beneficiary of your IRA, after you die, your estate will receive a charitable tax deduction for federal and state inheritance tax purposes of 10% of the account value when it is transferred into the CRUT, even though it may not be paid to the charity for years. Although the vast majority of estates do not have federal estate tax liability under the current laws, the tax deduction will reduce their state estate or inheritance tax liability, depending on whether their state of residence imposes an estate or inheritance tax.

What If I Have More than One Child?

First, there is no law saying that all children must be treated in exactly the same way. You could try to keep things relatively equal, but still have different plans for different children. The charitable trust might be a good solution for one child and a series of Roth IRA conversions, and no charitable trust might be the right solution for a different child.

Forgetting the world of charitable trusts for a moment, we often have one spendthrift and one or more responsible children. In that case, we name a spendthrift trust in lieu of leaving money to the spendthrift and leave the other siblings' money to them free of trust. There is no reason to draft and plan on maintaining unnecessary trusts. The treatment among the siblings might be different, but the goal is still equal treatment.

Let's assume you want to treat your children equally and with the same treatment. Some IRA owners might think a solution would be to name two or more lifetime beneficiaries of the CRUT. That is probably a good way to encourage fighting about money among siblings over the treatment of the trust after you are gone. It also reduces the amount the children get and increases the amount the charity gets because the life expectancy of two siblings is greater than one. Which means, when calculating how much goes to children and how much goes to charity, more money has to be preserved for the charity which reduces the children's income.

I would usually prefer having separate trusts, even knowing I am increasing accounting and trust maintenance costs. If you have two children, you could name each of them as the trustee of the other one's trust. That might change my million-dollar minimum preference, but perhaps $1,400,000 ($700,000 for each trust) because the work involved in maintaining two practically identical trusts is less than double the amount of maintaining one trust and there is an easy obvious choice of trustee.

Combining a Spendthrift Trust and the *"I Don't Want My No-Good Son-in-Law to Inherit One Red Cent of My Money"* Trust and a Charitable Trust

Before the SECURE Act, we drafted quite a few trusts for adult beneficiaries. A common issue we faced was when the adult child was a spendthrift. Leaving the child with a lot of money could be risky; rather than taking appropriate distributions and planning and investing wisely, there was the chance that the child would blow the money. In that situation, we typically left that money to a trust with the adult child as the beneficiary. We also provided the trustee with some discretion with respect to distributions of both income and principal. Having to protect a spendthrift adult from himself is not a new problem; it was around a long time ago and will likely always be a problem.

We also drafted trusts when there was a reasonable chance of the child developing or already having some type of liability. If your child had a judgment against him or was involved in a lawsuit and then inherited your after-tax dollars, he could lose that inheritance to his judgment creditor. (The person who sued your child and won.) The same would be true if your child inherited your IRA or Roth IRA. An inherited IRA or inherited Roth IRA does not enjoy the same creditor protection as an IRA or Roth IRA while you are alive. Therefore, any money, whether it be after-tax dollars, IRA or retirement plan dollars, Roth IRAs or any other funds that you want to leave to a child who has or potentially will have serious creditor issues should be left in a creditor protection trust for the benefit of that child.

On the other hand, if the IRA were left to a properly drafted trust, that money could be protected from the child's creditors and still provide income and support for the child. Sometimes we draft a trust "prophylactically." For example, the adult child is a brain surgeon. Doctors get sued all the time, and any money left to that child should likely be left in some type of creditor protection trust.

In addition, we are drafting more and more of a trust that we call the *"I Don't Want My No-Good Son-in-Law to Inherit One Red Cent of My Money"* trust. This trust protects your adult child from your future ex-son-in-law/daughter-in-law. That is, he is currently your son-in-law, but the potential is there for him to divorce your daughter after you die and go after at least a portion of the inheritance that you left to your daughter (to be fair, this example also extends to daughters-in-law). At a minimum, he will go after a portion of the appreciation of that money between your death and when they get divorced.

An alternative to the *"I Don't Want My No-Good Son-in-Law to Inherit One Red Cent of My Money"* trust is a postnuptial agreement between your daughter and son-in-law that would protect your inheritance. While great in theory, as a practical matter it is an excellent way to start a family fight. I prefer that wealthy parents discuss the value of prenuptial agreements with their children, preferably before an engagement and better yet before the child has even met their future spouse.

Well, for all three of these somewhat dire situations, a charitable remainder trust might be a great alternative solution. It would have all the creditor protections listed in the trusts above and might be a much smarter choice for reduced income taxes. The downside is that it does not allow for distributions for health, maintenance and support, so if there were years when the beneficiary needed more than the "income," they could not get it. Depending on the amount of the total estate to be allocated to the problem beneficiary, if there were a more traditional trust for non-IRA assets, money could be set aside there that would allow principal distributions for health, maintenance and support from the after-tax dollars.

Please note this charitable trust idea only works as a great tax strategy if the underlying asset is an IRA or retirement plan.

The Relationship Between Charitable Remainder Trusts and Roth IRA Conversions

In Chapter 14, we discuss the benefits of combining different strategies. For example, holding off on Social Security, doing a series of Roth IRA conversions, and having the fundamentals of Lange's Cascading Beneficiary Plan as your estate plan. That is a good example of combining different strategies that produce a synergistic positive result. That *might not* be the case with combining Roth IRA conversions and charitable remainder trusts.

Let's take the simple case where you project your traditional IRA will be about a million dollars or even less at your death. You like the idea of a series of Roth IRA conversions and you also like the idea of a charitable trust. So, you are thinking, maybe a little of each.

With those numbers, I don't like that combination. It doesn't make sense to name a charitable trust as the beneficiary of a Roth IRA. If you make a series of Roth IRA conversions, your Traditional IRA might be significantly lower than a million dollars at your death. Then, the cost of creating—but more importantly maintaining the CRUT after you die—becomes too high in relationship to the value of the CRUT. So, for IRA owners who project that they will have about a million dollars in their Traditional IRA at their death, I would likely either look to Roth IRA conversions or to a CRUT, but not both.

Combining CRUTs and Roth conversions have potential if you have or will have well over a million dollars in your Traditional IRA. Then you could make a series of Roth IRA conversions, name individuals as the beneficiary of your Roth

---

The warning, however, is that if you intend to name a CRUT as the beneficiary of your Traditional IRA, don't make so many Roth IRA conversions that the value of the Traditional IRA is worth well less than a million dollars at your death.

IRA, and still have a million dollars that you could allocate to the CRUT for the remaining Traditional IRA.

The warning, however, is that if you intend to name a CRUT as the beneficiary of your Traditional IRA, don't make so many Roth IRA conversions that the value of the Traditional IRA is worth well less than a million dollars at your death.

The point of this section is that a lot of IRA and retirement plan owners should pick either a Roth IRA conversion strategy or a CRUT strategy, but likely not both.

KEY IDEAS

- In many situations it would make more sense to leave your IRA or a portion of your IRA to a Charitable Remainder Trust than to leave it to your child directly.

  It is possible, even likely, that your child would actually end up with more money if you left the IRA to a charitable trust than if you left it to them outright.

- The Charitable Remainder Trust also has the same benefits of other creditor protection trusts.

- Depending on how much money you have in your IRA, it may be appropriate to either go the Charitable Remainder Trust route or the Roth IRA conversion route, but not both.

- Charitable Trusts have advantages and disadvantages that have to be assessed on an individual basis.

Which Dollars You Should Leave to Charity?

"You must pay taxes. But there's no law that says you gotta leave a tip."

— Morgan Stanley

This chapter, though short, will point out an expensive mistake that the vast majority of IRA and retirement plan owners make when they leave money to charity. The good news is that this mistake is easily remedied.

Let's forget about trusts for the moment and concentrate on a really basic mistake. It will seem obvious after you read it, but again, it is probably a mistake you are currently making with the money you intend to go to charity.

Assume you have an estate consisting of $500,000 in an IRA and $500,000 in after-tax money. Assume further that you want half of your estate to go to charity and the other half to go to your heirs. (Please stay with this example even if your charitable instinct is far more modest.) Many planners, in an attempt to keep things simple, would prepare wills and beneficiary designations leaving one-half of the IRA and one-half of the after-tax funds to the charity and the rest to the heirs. Or worse, they would leave the entire IRA to the heirs and make a bequest of the after-tax money to charity.

The key point here is charities don't care in what form (IRA, after-tax, highly appreciated dollars, Roth IRA, etc.) they get their money because they do not pay income taxes. Individuals do care because of the different tax implications of the distinct types of inherited funds.

Under most circumstances, it now makes sense to leave IRA or retirement money to charity because the charity will not pay taxes on the bequests. In the past, if the beneficiary of the IRA was age 40 or younger, the advantages of the stretch IRA sometimes outweighed the fact that income taxes would be due on the distributions. That is, the ability to "stretch" the Inherited IRA more than made up for the fact that the beneficiary would have to eventually pay taxes on the total distributions from the inherited IRA.

Previously, so many decisions as to whom you should leave what money were age dependent. For a beneficiary age 41 or older, I usually recommended that he or she inherit the after-tax funds and that the charity receive the IRA. For someone 40 or younger who planned to stretch the IRA by limiting distributions to the minimum, I used to recommend that he or she receive the Inherited IRA and that the charity receive the after-tax funds. In either case, the charity doesn't care because it is all the same to them.

However, with the death of the stretch IRA, planning for family members becomes simpler in this one area. Ultimately, it will likely make more sense to leave IRAs and retirement accounts to charity, since they will be of less value to the family with the death of the stretch.

A more typical example is someone who has more than a million dollars in their IRA who would like to make a $100,000 bequest to a charity. Practically every estate plan we see that comes in from the outside, even those drafted by the expensive downtown estate attorneys who work for big firms, designates that the $100,000 should come from money outside the IRA instead of from the IRA. We see these bequests in wills and revocable trusts.

That's just thoughtless, and these bigshot attorneys ought to know better. The money intended for charity should be specified via the beneficiary designation of your IRA or retirement plan; this is money that, if left to your heirs, would come with an income-tax bill.

Let's go through the steps one more time. Leaving $100,000 from your will or revocable trust of after-tax dollars to a charity reduces the family inheritance by $100,000. But if you leave $100,000 to a charity as part of the beneficiary designation of your IRA or retirement plan, meaning you are leaving pre-tax or IRA money to charity, your family wins because of the tax implications.

As we have said, the charity pays no taxes, but your children would have to pay taxes. So, the $100,000 IRA left to your heirs would be taxed—as much as 40%—leaving them with $60,000 instead of the $100,000 of after-tax investments. That is significant. If your documents include this mistake, please make the necessary changes. If you are anticipating a larger contribution, the tax savings of getting this right could be substantially more.

For anyone considering charitable donations, for 2020 the CARES Act temporarily increases the federal income tax deduction for donations up to 100% of a taxpayer's AGI. The prior limit was 60%, which will resume in 2021. In the next chapter we cover yet another important way to combine charitable giving and tax abatement: Qualified Charitable Distributions (QCDs). The rules for QCDs require that the donor be at least age 70½, so it is not a strategy available to everyone. We would also like to recognize Steven T. Kohman, CPA, CSEP, CSRP, our senior accountant and master number runner, for all the research and writing of Chapter 10.

10

Qualified Charitable Distribution (QCD) Rules Save Extra Money on Charitable Donations

by Steve Kohman, *CPA, CSEP, CSRP*

"As you grow older, you will discover that you have two hands: one for helping yourself, the other for helping others."

— **Sam Levenson,** *In One Era & Out the Other*

Most readers who are over age 70½ will have a Traditional IRA and many will make some donations to charity. If this describes you, you should be glad to know that the Qualified Charitable Distribution (QCD) rules are now permanent tax laws, and we can safely put them to use.

QCD Rules and Limitations

A QCD is a method for donating to charity directly from your IRA. Also, it only applies to distributions from IRAs, not from other retirement plans like 401(k)s or 403(b)s.

The QCD rules require you to be age 70½. When the QCD laws were established, you had to begin taking required minimum distributions (RMDs) by age 70½. Despite the fact that the SECURE Act raised the RMD age to 72, they didn't change the QCD laws. Therefore, previously (and even now) if you were making QCDs before you turned 72, your charitable contribution coming directly from your IRA counted as at least part of your required minimum distribution. Now, for example if you are age 71, you can still make a QCD even though you aren't required to take an RMD.

Under the QCD rules, you can make charitable donations directly from your IRA. The withdrawal from the IRA is not taxable, but you also do not receive a charitable deduction. This is in contrast to taking a taxable distribution from your IRA, paying income tax on that distribution, and giving money to a qualifying charity [a 501(c)(3)] and claiming that contribution as a charitable donation on your itemized deductions.

QCDs cannot be claimed as a charitable donation on your itemized deductions. People often think making a charitable donation through a QCD will not make any difference in their taxes and, in some cases, it might not make a significant difference if you itemize deductions. In many cases, however, it creates significant savings. Furthermore, since the 2020 and beyond standard deduction is so much higher than it was before 2019 and since there are now so many more significant restrictions on what itemized deductions are allowed, it is more likely that taxpayers who used to itemize their deductions will not itemize deductions anymore. For the people who used to itemize but no longer can, QCDs provide a terrific way to save on taxes.

The QCD rules limit the types of charities that can receive QCD donations. Donations to donor advised funds, private foundations, or a supporting organization under IRS Section 509(a)(3) are not permitted. Unfortunately, this means that donations to a Fidelity Charitable Giving account or Vanguard Charitable or any other donor advised fund cannot be used for QCDs. However, most other 501(c)(3) charities do qualify.

The QCD rules limit these direct IRA donations to charity to $100,000 per year per person. If you are married, both spouses can donate up to $100,000 each, or $200,000 total.

For people with basis[7] in their IRAs, using QCDs will not use your basis on the amount donated to charity. This is another advantage of QCDs. (You would have basis in your IRAs if you or an employer made a retirement plan contribution in which you did not receive a tax benefit. A non-deductible IRA would be one common example.)

Even if you do itemize, the advantages of using QCDs is that you lower your taxable IRA income and thus lower your Adjusted Gross Income (AGI) shown on your tax return. If you only take the required distribution from your IRAs and you use a QCD, you will only be taxed on the remainder of your RMD after the

---

[7] IRA basis is the funds in an IRA that already have been taxed, either as nondeductible IRA contributions or after-tax funds rolled over from plans.

charitable contribution. This provides many money saving advantages in various tax situations as discussed next.

Savings When the Standard Deduction is Used

The "home run" created by QCDs is for people who take the standard deduction and do not use itemized deductions. The standard deduction is $27,400 (married, filing jointly, and over age 65) for 2020. Combining the higher itemized deduction and the extreme limitations on other itemized deductions like taxes paid, many more taxpayers will use the standard deduction than ever before. QCDs will reduce the AGI on your tax return, and since the standard deduction is not affected, it lowers the taxable income and lowers your taxes. For example, if you donate $10,000 to charity, use the standard deduction, and you are in the 24% tax bracket, using QCDs will save you $2,400.

Savings on Medicare Premiums

Nearly all people age 70½ are on Medicare. The premiums for Part B and sometimes Part D are usually deducted from their Social Security payments. If your Modified AGI (MAGI, which includes tax-exempt interest) is over a certain amount, these Medicare premiums will be raised for one year in the future.

For example, using 2020 rules for married couples the first threshold is $174,000 of MAGI. If the couple's MAGI was $176,000 in 2018, the 2020 Medicare premiums would be increased for each spouse by $57.80 per month for Part B and $12.20 per month for Part D. This is $1,680 extra cost for 2020. If you were going to have just over $174,000 of MAGI, using QCDs to lower your MAGI below that amount would provide a great savings—at no real cost if you planned to donate to charity anyway.

There are additional 2020 thresholds of increased Medicare premiums at MAGI levels of $218,000; $272,000; $326,000 and $750,000. The increases in Medicare premiums B and D are larger at each of these thresholds and are $2,546.40 more at each threshold for 2020 for a married couple using both Parts B and D. Using QCDs to get under these thresholds saves even more money.

Improved Roth IRA Strategy

QCDs can help in the Roth conversion planning process. Some people want to make Roth conversions but only up to the point where their Medicare premiums will not increase based on MAGI. Since MAGI is reduced by using QCDs, more can be converted to Roth IRAs. Others want to make Roth IRA conversions up to, but not to exceed a certain tax bracket, often 24%. QCDs can lower your income and increase the amount you can convert to a Roth IRA and stay within your desired tax bracket.

Various Other Benefits of QCDs

Without getting too much more involved in the tax code, there are many other ways QCDs can benefit you by reducing your AGI. Certain deductions and credits are limited by higher AGI. *A tax credit example* is the lifetime learning credit for retirees who are taking some college courses later in life. Using QCDs may help you qualify for the credit. *A deduction example* is the rental loss deduction that can become limited if your income is over certain amounts. Using QCDs lowers your income and may allow a larger rental loss deduction.

No Downside or Costs of QCDs?

The minimal downsides of using QCDs are simply the procedures. There is no cost to using them. Usually, you must only send your IRA investment manager or broker the name and address of the charity and how much to donate. You will likely want to lower your other RMDs above the amount donated, so keep track of this. You will still need to get the documentation letters from the charities as you would with any other charitable donation. You will have to keep track of the QCDs and tell your tax preparer you made them. If you prepare your own tax return, you must follow the rules on how to present the QCDs on Form 1040.

It may add a slight burden on the IRA broker to process a QCD distribution. Because of the additional paperwork, you may want to use QCDs only for larger contribution amounts. You may even want to "bunch-up" your charitable donations for the year, or even for two years at a time, to take advantage of the standard deduction and other advantages mentioned above.

I have heard of at least one brokerage account that will give you a checkbook for your IRA and you can write a check directly to the charitable organization. I know some providers don't like this technique and I am not certain this will work, but it sure seems to simplify life for the IRA owner, even if not the advisor or broker.

Use QCDs!

Because there are no significant disadvantages and no costs for using QCDs, you should use them to make your charitable donations if you are over age 70.5.

If it is early in the tax year, you may not even be aware of how they will save you money for the current year.

I know this is a lot of technical information, and it is a shame the IRS makes you "jump through hoops" for QCDs instead of just allowing you deduct all your charitable donations from IRA income. But why not take a small jump and find out from your tax advisor if you would see any potential savings. It certainly makes sense if you were going to make the charitable donations anyway!

KEY IDEAS

- People often think making a charitable donation through a QCD will not make any difference in their taxes and, in some cases, it might not make a significant difference if you itemize deductions.

  In many cases, however, it creates significant savings.

- Because there are no significant disadvantages and no costs for using QCDs, you should use them to make your charitable donations if you are over age 70½.

"Retire Secure Initial Consultation" — yours FREE!

On January 1, 2020, the SECURE Act took effect. It now forces your IRA and other retirement plans to be fully distributed and taxed within 10 years of your passing. So, all the wealth you worked so hard to earn during your lifetime can be taxed away in one short decade—leaving your heirs with absolutely nothing to show for it!

But, as an owner of this book, you may qualify for a FREE, no-obligation **Retire Secure Initial Consultation** (value: $997) introducing you to proven tax-saving strategies—including Roth IRA conversions, gifting, life insurance, **Lange's Cascading Beneficiary Plan**, sprinkle trusts, CRUTs, and asset allocation—to keep your legacy wealth in your family's hands ... and out of Uncle Sam's.

All 100% legal, so it won't raise an eyebrow at the IRS.

To see whether you qualify* for a FREE *Retire Secure Consultation* with **Lange Financial Group** via phone or Zoom, call us toll-free at **1-800-387-1129** or go to page **175**.

But we urge you to hurry: I can only handle so many *Retire Secure Consultations*. Appointments are made first if I think we are a good fit to work together and second on a first-come, first-service basis.

* You must have $1 million or more of investable assets that you would consider placing under management with Lange Financial Group—assuming you like our retirement planning and tax-saving strategies as well as our money manager and his process and investments.

11

The Sprinkle Trust: Another Tool in the Estate Planner's Toolbox

"Money is like muck—not good except it be spread."

— Francis Bacon

What Are Sprinkle Trusts and How/When are They Appropriate?

Sprinkle trusts used in an optimal manner could now provide families with the opportunity to spread the tax burden from Inherited IRAs among multiple generations by including children, grandchildren, and even great-grandchildren. They could also be used to protect beneficiaries in vulnerable life situations by retaining the income for their benefit in the trust. Sprinkle trusts have been one of the many "tools" in the sophisticated estate planner's repertoire for years, but now they will become much more attractive because they can provide significant tax benefits. To be fair, there are also major disadvantages associated with these trusts.

Before analyzing the advantages and disadvantages, it is helpful to understand what a sprinkle trust is. A sprinkle trust is created under a will or a living trust and can distribute its income among a group of beneficiaries at the discretion of the trustee. Using a sprinkle trust with Traditional IRAs is particularly attractive under the new law because of the opportunity to spread the taxable IRA income among children, grandchildren, great-grandchildren, nieces, nephews, etc. Think of a sprinkle trust as an opportunity to stretch income among multiple beneficiaries with the additional flexibility of having the trust pay the income tax for a young or spendthrift beneficiary. In other situations, it might be best

to maintain Inherited IRAs in the trust even if the rate would be higher on the taxable income retained in the trust than the income tax rate of the beneficiary.

To use a sprinkle trust for an IRA, the beneficiary designation must name the trust as a beneficiary. The trust can be a partial beneficiary of the IRA or the only beneficiary. In addition, the trust can be a primary beneficiary or a contingent beneficiary. Once the IRA is inherited by the sprinkle trust, the trustee will have to withdraw all the money in the IRA over 10 years. The trustee could wait the full 10 years to withdraw the money, but it will likely make sense to withdraw the income annually to smooth out the income as much as possible.

Once withdrawn, the trustee can choose whether to retain the income in the trust or pay it to the beneficiary. If retained, the trust pays tax on the income at very high rates, with the top marginal tax rate of 37% kicking in at approximately $12,000 of retained income. If distributed, each beneficiary pays income tax on their distribution. In most cases, distribution will be favorable, but trustees will have to rely on tax advice to minimize triggering kiddie tax on distributions to young beneficiaries (i.e., grandchildren, great-nephews, great-nieces, etc.).

Stretching the income over multiple beneficiaries at the discretion of the trustee can be a great solution for minimizing income taxes on the IRA and maximizing its value to the family. However, the sprinkle trust solution has its drawbacks.

First, you are asking the trustee to demonstrate the wisdom of King Solomon in an attempt to develop a masterplan for the trust and to make the optimal distribution for the benefit of each beneficiary. Second, you are putting tremendous strain on the fiduciary duty that a trustee owes to the beneficiaries by forcing the trustee to choose which beneficiaries (their children or their siblings or their nieces and nephews in many circumstances) should receive the IRA distributions. Finally, there is the inevitable complexity of a trust with its tax returns and the question among family members of why their loved one just did not give the IRA directly to them in the first place.

So, our recommendation is to approach the sprinkle trust with extreme caution but to consider it as a possible beneficiary of some portion of an IRA in cases where beneficiaries would be better not getting money directly by virtue of maturity, age, marital situation, creditor protection, mental disability, government benefits, etc. In addition, because of the complexities of the sprinkle trust, it will probably make the most sense for IRA owners to consider this solution for larger IRA accounts, where their beneficiaries would not otherwise have the discipline to take out the IRA over 10 years to minimize their income tax.

Now, we will take a look at gifting as a strategy to mitigate the death of the stretch IRA.

KEY IDEAS

- A sprinkle trust is created under a will or a living trust and can distribute its income among a group of beneficiaries at the discretion of the trustee.

- A sprinkle trust allows the trustee to stretch income among multiple beneficiaries with the additional flexibility of having the trust pay the income tax for a young or spendthrift beneficiary.

- Sprinkle trusts can be onerous for trustees who have to make tough decisions about who gets what when.

"Retire Secure Initial Consultation" — yours FREE!

On January 1, 2020, the SECURE Act took effect. It now forces your IRA and other retirement plans to be fully distributed and taxed within 10 years of your passing. As Table 2.1 (please see page 37) shows, this accelerated taxation can, in combination with cash withdrawals, mean the difference of your child having $2,000,000 later in life compared to being broke.

But, as an owner of this book, you may qualify for a FREE, no-obligation **Retire Secure Initial Consultation** (value: $997) introducing you to proven tax-saving strategies—including Roth IRA conversions, **Lange's Cascading Beneficiary Plan**, gifting, CRUTs, sprinkle trusts, gifting—to keep your legacy wealth in your family's hands ... and out of Uncle Sam's.

All 100% legal, so it won't raise an eyebrow at the IRS.

To see whether YOU qualify* for a FREE *Retire Secure Consultation* with **Lange Financial Group**, call us toll-free at **1-800-387-1129** or look at the back of the book on page **175**. No need to drive to our Pittsburgh offices or even go outside. To help keep you safe from COVID-19, we are currently conducting all consultations virtually via phone or Zoom conference!

Appointments are made first if I think we are a good fit to work together and second on a first-come, first-service basis.

---

* You must have $1 million or more of investable assets that you would consider placing under management with Lange Financial Group—assuming you like our retirement planning and tax-saving strategies as well as our money manager and his process and investments.

12

Gifting and Spending Strategies to Combat the Death of the Stretch IRA

"We make a living by what we get. We make a life by what we give."

— **Winston Churchill**

The Big Picture with Gifting to Families for Many of My Clients and Readers

Most of my clients and my prospective clients are looking for guidance on things like reducing taxes, Roth IRA conversions, asset allocation, the best estate plan, saving and spending strategies to never run out of money, and other things covered in this book. Of course, our office and the firms we work with try to do our best in these areas. But sometimes, these areas don't reflect the way we can provide the most value to clients and their families.

I can't tell you the number of people I consult with whose family could benefit from a gifting plan.

When I meet with a client or a prospective client, I genuinely try to listen two thirds of the time and talk one third of the time. As you can imagine, that isn't always easy for me. I also try to address what the client says is their biggest concern. But of course, I will eventually bring up what I think a client should have as part of their plan. It is often a gifting plan.

I met a single older woman who had a $35 million estate. She was spending roughly $10,000/month. She had children and grandchildren with financial needs. She was facing a massive federal estate tax liability. Aggressive gifting would have reduced her estate tax liability by millions. It would also have had the benefit of helping her family when they were younger and needed the money before rather than after she died.

After a discussion of the type of things you would expect, I brought up the idea of giving some of her money to her family members now. I had significant gifting in mind but was hoping and even expecting to convince her make at least some gifts. Her response: "What if I get sick?"

OK, so you are laughing. Are you sure that you aren't at least a little bit guilty of that same type of thinking?

Of course, I am never going to advocate gifting to family members if it would threaten your or your spouse's financial security. I am extremely conservative about estimating how much money you will need and always err on the high side. Plus, I like to factor in provisions for long-term care and other emergency buffers. I also factor in an additional market drop. I even add in an optimistic projection that you will start spending more than you currently spend.

But what if I do all that and there is *still a lot of excess money.* I start thinking in terms of gifting, even if it isn't even on my client's radar.

The goal of life, and even good financial planning for that matter, is not to see who dies with the most money.

Obviously, the explicit plan is to optimize most of the things we have been talking about, Roth IRA conversions, wills and trusts and beneficiary designations, investments, and asset allocation, etc.

I also understand you are justifiably reluctant to gift after the downturn in the market after COVID-19. As I mentioned earlier, my wife is nervous about spending money now. But what if, based on current assets and income, even using the most conservative assumptions, our projections show that your estate will grow and grow and grow?

Without any lifetime gifting, all assets will be left to the surviving spouse at the first death. Ultimately, when the second spouse dies, sometime in their 80s or 90s, and the kids are in their 60s, there would be a massive tax on the sizable estate. In addition, the children would not have had the benefit of the family money when they were younger and needed the money much more. This makes a compelling case for making gifts.

Furthermore, think about this for a minute. For many if not most of my clients and readers, if you inherited an extra $100,000 today, it wouldn't make much of a difference in your life. But what if you had inherited $100,000 (even adjusted for inflation) thirty years ago? What kind of difference would it have made then?

I had another client with $3,000,000. He spent $7,500/month. It was reasonable to project that with his Social Security, he would die with a lot more money than he has now. He was never married and didn't have any kids. His sister, who he was close with, was too sick to work, had run up her credit cards, and was barely getting by with Social Security and a tiny pension. She lived in financial gloom. When he saw me for a review and I learned of this situation, I suggested he give his sister $100,000. Much to my surprise, he did it.

That $100,000 gift truly did not have any significant impact on my client's finances. He didn't change his behavior one bit. He didn't eat out one more or less time. He didn't take one more or less vacation. The gift did, however, make a life changing difference for his sister. It was also life changing for my client because he felt so good about the gift.

The goal of life, and even good financial planning for that matter, is not to see who dies with the most money.

Gifting More than $15,000 per Year (or $30,000 if Married)

You might ask how could my client have made a $100,000 gift when the annual exclusion is only $15,000 per beneficiary ($30,000 if you are married and your spouse joins in the gift)? To make the math easy, please assume he gave $115,000 to his sister. Yes, theoretically there would be a gift tax on the extra $100,000 of the gift. However, assuming you file the appropriate gift tax return on Form US 709, you can elect to have the $100,000 subtracted from your lifetime gifting exemption instead of paying gift taxes on the gift currently.

What happens if you do that? That means if you are single, you would have to subtract $100,000 from your $11,580,000 federal exemption to arrive at a reduced federal exemption for estate tax purposes of $11,480,00. That means if your estate doesn't exceed $11,480,000 at your death (or $23,060,000 if you are married), there will be no federal gift tax, estate tax or transfer tax.

True, the exclusion is likely to come down in future years but because of the anti-clawback rules that we will not cover here, there is even more of an incentive to make a big gift now if you are trying to avoid federal gift or estate taxes. In addition, you are also getting the appreciation on the gift from the time of the gift to your death out of your estate. Finally, even if there are no federal transfer tax differences, there could be substantial state inheritance tax savings with large gifts.

If, after running a series of long-term financial projections using a series of very conservative assumptions, there is sufficient money to make gifts, you should strongly consider a formal gifting program.

How a Gift Can Continue Giving

Another way to tackle the problem of accelerated taxes on IRAs is to bestow gifts on family members via regular taxed withdrawals from your IRA. Not indiscriminately, but with tax advantages in mind both for you and the recipient using use one of the "leveraged gifting" techniques to be described. This strategy slowly reduces the amount in your traditional IRA and leaves less to face the "death tax" burden. Plus, it can confer significant advantages to your children while they are still young.

Of course, gifting can take on many flavors. It could be a straight-forward gift, "Here is some money." It could be a contribution to a 529 plan (tax-free college funding mechanism). It could provide money that your beneficiaries might use to contribute to their own Roth IRAs. It could even pay for premiums on a life insurance policy on the life of the IRA owner and spouse, the proceeds of which are tax-free.

One way to buy a life insurance policy for you and your spouse would be to cash in a portion of your IRA, pay the taxes on the distribution and use the remainder to buy a life insurance policy. This classic technique, known as pension rescue, generally involves taking a withdrawal that amounts to between 1 and 2% of the value of the IRA, paying income taxes on that withdrawal and then using the net proceeds to pay the life insurance premium.

When we say life insurance, we *are not talking* about life insurance for a surviving spouse or for minor children who will need support should the wage earner or wage earners die prematurely. In this instance, we are talking about types of permanent life insurance that guarantee a death benefit, assuming you make your premium payments.

Simply put, if you need to protect the income of one or two wage earners, usually the best way to do this is with laddered term insurance. While extremely important, that is an entirely different topic and is not covered in this book.

(Please see *Retire Secure!*, Third Edition, p. 28 for a detailed description of my recommendations for those who need term life insurance but want to keep their premiums to a minimum.)

I consider gifting, or life insurance some of the most tax-and cost-efficient methods of transferring wealth to your heirs. If you have a lot of money in retirement plans, a life insurance plan can not only get your beneficiaries more money, but it can also provide them with additional liquidity. It can also provide the tax-free dollars needed to pay income taxes that will be due on Inherited IRA withdrawals, essentially leaving the asset intact for as long as the law allows. Without the life insurance, your heirs may have to withdraw additional money from the IRA just to pay the tax due on the withdrawals, causing more tax, and ultimately forcing more and more money out of the tax-deferred environment. The combination of life insurance and charitable techniques, including the CRUT discussed earlier is a powerful combination.

But for our purposes now, I am talking about life insurance as one type of gift to your children. If you don't think that you can afford to give your heirs a gift of any kind, then you should not give them gifts, and you should not consider buying life insurance to make their situation easier.

If, however, you can afford to make gifts to your family, I am a huge fan of four basic types of gifts.

1. A plain old, no-strings-attached gift.
2. A gift for a specific purpose, i.e., here is $30,000 for the down payment on a house or even a gift to fund a Roth IRA for a child or grandchild. Technically, there should be no "strings" on a qualifying gift, but sometimes the purpose of the gift can be hinted at.
3. The gift of education for grandchildren in the form of Section 529 plans or even direct tuition gifts.
4. Permanent (not Term) Life insurance.

You're probably familiar with the first three types of gifts, so I won't dwell on them. Using one of the first three gifting techniques mentioned above after withdrawing money from a Traditional IRA is one way to reduce the value of an Inherited Traditional IRA that will be taxed within 10 years of your death. When used properly, the fourth type of gift, life insurance, has a number of benefits that make it an excellent part of the best possible wealth transfer strategy. The proceeds from life insurance are free from income tax, and if set up properly, free from estate, inheritance, and transfer taxes.

Considering that several of the members of our firm are licensed to sell life insurance, both my office and I have sold an incredibly small number of life insurance policies over the years. One reason is I preferred that clients take advantage of the first three types of gifts listed above. I was not opposed to life insurance, but I wasn't passionate about it. I did recognize the value when we "ran the numbers" under the old law, but it wasn't one of the first things I would think about to optimize a client's estate plan. With the SECURE Act now law, my thinking has shifted significantly in favor in insurance.

In the past, when we did recommend life insurance to help preserve an estate, more often than not we recommended a Second-to-Die life insurance policy for owners of large IRAs who could afford the premium. This type of policy pays a benefit upon the death of the second spouse. The premiums are substantially lower than individual policies on one or both spouses because the life insurance company won't have to pay the proceeds until both are deceased.

When we "ran the numbers," purchasing life insurance made sense for a lot of families.

Life insurance is no better now than before the SECURE Act. But if the alternative is leaving a lot of money in an IRA which will suffer massive income tax acceleration under the SECURE Act, then this is an issue to evaluate. So, I reran the numbers using current law and the results from buying a Second-to-Die policy are impressive.

If income tax rates go up in the future, buying life insurance will work out even better for your children than the alternative of you not buying the insurance. The reason is the kids will be getting income and estate and inheritance tax-free money versus the alternative of inheriting a bigger IRA which will be subject to the ten-year rule for income tax acceleration and, depending on where you live, inheritance taxes on top of income taxes.

Here's an example. Let's say that you buy a $1 million Second-to-Die life insurance policy, and the premiums are $20,000 every year. Fifteen years later, both you and your spouse have passed. You've paid $300,000 in premiums, but your children are going to get a check from your insurance company for $1 million. That's a $700,000 gain, and it's income, inheritance and capital gain tax-free.

Since the SECURE Act we are also examining polices on the life of one spouse. Then, with the proceeds we are making Roth IRA conversions after the first spouse dies. Depending on the situation, that might be better than doing Roth IRA conversions now and buying a Second-to-Die life insurance policy.

If you decide an insurance solution should be part of your overall plan, my recommendation would be to be conservative in the amount of coverage that you buy, so that you and your spouse will always be comfortable with the premium. Different situations require different solutions. In addition, life insurance isn't always a pure numbers decision.

Sometimes life insurance can be looked at as a guaranteed investment that, given a normal or even long life, offers a great income-tax free return on your investment and is one form of a guaranteed investment. It is particularly appropriate if you want a child or children to receive a certain amount of money no matter what happens to the stock market.

The other issue is, even if life insurance is indicated, different types of policies will work well in some situations and others will work better in other situations. Personal preferences for how and when you want your money distributed also come into play. Also, please remember that life insurance should be only one component of your gifting strategy. It should be in addition to, not in place of, the three other types of gifts mentioned above.

Taking money from your IRA, paying the taxes, and then using that money to buy life insurance or a 529 plan or even a Roth IRA for your children is conceptually similar to making a Roth IRA conversion. In all instances you are paying income taxes now in return for tax-free growth in the future. In all three instances there is the additional bonus that, if handled correctly, they will escape all transfer and estate taxes. That said, Roth IRA conversions, life insurance, 529 plans, and other gifting techniques should not be competing strategies, but complementary strategies.

Quantifying the Benefits of Life Insurance

So, what do some of the numbers look like? Let's compare two families with identical finances, interest rate, taxes, etc. The only difference is one buys a Second-to-Die policy and the other family does not. Using reasonable assumptions found in the Appendix the result, over their lifetimes the children of the couple with insurance will have $2,000,000 more than the children of the couple that didn't buy life insurance.

Life insurance should be only one component of your gifting strategy. It should be in addition to, not in place of, the three other types of gifts mentioned above.

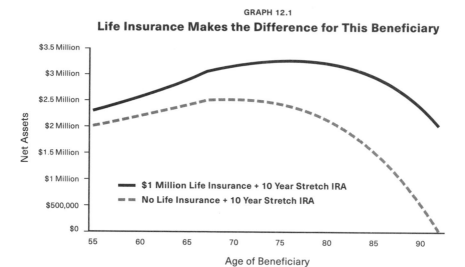

GRAPH 12.1

Life Insurance Makes the Difference for This Beneficiary

Please see detailed assumptions in the Appendix.

If you don't gift or buy life insurance, your beneficiaries are forced to pay the taxes on your IRA within 10 years and the effects could be devastating. This graph shows that buying life insurance can go a long way toward minimizing those effects and preserving your wealth for future generations. The next question is, when is the best time to buy? A Chinese proverb says the best time to plant a tree is twenty years ago. The second-best time is now. If you think that buying life insurance might make sense for you, you should look into it as soon as possible. The generally accepted rule of thumb for life insurance is to get the insurance while you are still insurable. Unexpected health problems in the future may cause insurance companies to reject you or rate your health so badly that the premium will be too expensive to consider seriously.

An Alternative to Long-Term Care Insurance

As long as we are talking about insurance, I am much less a fan of long-term care insurance (LTC) than most financial professionals. One of the problems with LTC is that the premiums are not guaranteed, and historically buyers have suffered huge increases after the date of purchase. Another problem is that if you never need LTC, you have paid all those premiums, and other than peace of mind, received no benefit.

A reasonable alternative to a traditional LTC policy is to get a combination LTC and life insurance policy. Technically, this is a life insurance policy with an LTC rider.

Let's assume you purchase a $500,000 combination LTC and life insurance policy. Let's also assume that you never need care, and you die. Your heirs will get the full $500,000 death benefit. Now let's assume you need $250,000 of care (after the deductible). The insurance company pays for your care and when you die, your heirs are paid $250,000. Finally, let's say you need $600,000 worth of care. The insurance company pays the first $500,000, and you are on the hook for the other $100,000.

Another nice feature of this combination policy is that the proceeds for LTC insurance are, under current law, tax-free. And since it is a life insurance policy with an LTC rider, it may be easier for you to qualify for coverage at a more favorable rating, than for traditional LTC coverage. A more detailed discussion of the combination LTC and life insurance policy is a different topic for a different day, but something I prefer for most clients to traditional LTC if both LTC and life insurance are needed.

Personally, I have a term policy on my life because my wife and daughter would need to replace my income if I died prematurely. I also have a combination life and LTC policy on my life. My wife has a combination life and LTC policy on her life. We also have a Second-to-Die life insurance policy. We have also converted most of our traditional retirement plans to Roth IRA or Roth 401(k)s. We also have our money invested in Dimensional Fund Advisor (DFA) enhanced index funds. So, for what it is worth, I practice what I preach!

If you can afford to make gifts and life insurance isn't an appropriate solution in your case, then you should consider making other types of gifts. In addition to the types of gifts mentioned above, consider one more idea to protect yourself from the death of the stretch IRA.

Spend More Money

Spend more money! Even in the face of COVID-19, if you can afford it, spend some money. To be honest, I have been only moderately successful in my efforts to convince clients to spend more money, even when they can easily afford it. Even if they intellectually understand the math and calculations behind the recommendations we make, few of my clients who are age 65 or older are great spenders relative to their income and net worth. At least for the moment, I will not try to change your leopard's spots.

That said, my favorite way to spend your money, and where I have been persuasive with many clients, is to recommend that you sponsor a family vacation. My father-in-law hosts a family vacation every year and picks up the tab for the entire family. For a four-day weekend, the entire family drives or flies into a resort in the Poconos (a recreational area in the mountains of Pennsylvania). All the kids and grandchildren and now great-grandchildren come and hang out together to play games, swim at the pool, laugh at the Comedy Club, and enjoy different family activities. We all eat three meals a day together in the dining room.

My daughter, Erica, an only child who is now 25 years old, knows all of her cousins well, and they are in frequent contact on Facebook. She would not have this sense of being part of a bigger family were it not for these annual family gatherings. As we go to press, a lot of people are staying home, and my daughter has been having a blast chatting online with her cousins. When my father-in-law passes, he will leave a little less money to his family, but he will have provided the priceless legacy of strengthened family bonds and sense of clan even though we live all over the country.

This advice, incidentally, is consistent with multiple other authors who say, "buy experiences, don't buy things." Obviously, in the face of COVID-19, it may not be safe to sponsor family gatherings, but I think you see the point.

I will also mention some suggestions for spending that a lot of clients take notice of when I mention them, but usually don't do them. They are especially important in the face of living through the COVID-19 crisis. I do everything in the list that follows.

- My family has a nutritionist and a private chef to design and cook our meals.
- We have a concierge physician.
- We have a maid service and a laundry service.
- We have a personal trainer who used to come to our house three mornings a week. Now he trains us virtually.
- I have two e-bikes and two regular bicycles.
- I receive stem cell treatments every year for psoriatic arthritis (they have really helped me).

The following are things I used to spend money on and hope to again someday:

- We don't hesitate to travel whenever we want.
- We eat out whenever we want.
- I use Uber a lot, even though I am perfectly capable of driving.
- I get the best seats I can for concerts and shows.

The vast majority of my clients, many of whom are significantly wealthier than I am, don't do these things. They, and frankly many of my readers, probably regard these things as extravagant. But I think if you factor in quality of life, it might be wise to consider adopting some of them. For many clients adopting even just a few of these quality of life enhancers might mean the difference between dying with $3.2 million instead of $3.4 million, but the added enjoyment and gained quality of life will be well worth it. It is worth thinking about.

I don't say these things to brag. I have a lot of clients who could easily afford everything on this list and a lot more. We like to calculate how much money clients can afford to spend without ever running out of money. Depending on your situation and how much you want or need to leave behind, chances are that it is really OK to spend more than you are right now, even in the face of COVID-19 and the related recession.

I am not saying to spend frivolously. You would not be where you are today if you did. As an example, though I am extravagant in some areas, I have never paid to fly first class. My wife and I drive old fully-paid-up Subarus. My wife, who has a master's degree in electrical engineering from Carnegie Mellon University, and my daughter are both much thriftier than I.

True, I work long hours and I am in the prime of my career in terms of productivity and earning capacity. One rationalization for this relatively lavish lifestyle is that I am buying time; I can make more money per hour working than doing some of the things on the list. That said, I am also buying health. To be fair, I have only spent like this in very recent years. I should also mention that even though my income will be reduced quite a bit because of the business impact of COVID-19, I have not curtailed my spending.

I mention these things to get you to consider adding one or two of them or something else that you think would improve your quality of life. I doubt you will miss the money.

For many clients adopting even just a few of these quality of life enhancers might mean the difference between dying with $3.2 million instead of $3.4 million, but the added enjoyment and gained quality of life will be well worth it ...
It is worth thinking about.

> **My favorite way to spend your money, and where I have been persuasive with many clients, is to recommend that you sponsor a family vacation.**

Allow me to offer something I just sent out in my hard copy newsletter.

In previous communications, I have encouraged clients to spend more money on taking care of themselves. Buying organic food, getting a nutritionist/ health coach, hiring a concierge doctor, hiring a virtual physical trainer and more. I believe all these things will bring you a higher return than the market even in good times.

Finally, one more personal note. I got a lot more personal satisfaction from talking the man into giving his sister $100,000 than coming up with a perfect Roth IRA conversion plan that might save a family a million dollars.

The point of this chapter, however, is to show you that additional spending, making gifts to your family and purchasing life insurance can increase the quality of your and your family's life and be a great hedge against the SECURE Act.

KEY IDEAS

- Gifting and life insurance are two of the most tax and cost-efficient methods of transferring wealth to your heirs.
- Be conservative in the amount of life insurance that you buy, so that you and your spouse will always be comfortable with the premium and you have money in your gifting budget for other types of gifts.
- Gifts and life insurance can be a great hedge against the law taxing IRAs.

Retirement and Estate Planning—Once Difficult, Now Easy!

Often, we hear from readers of our books who tell us, "I am intrigued by the well-thought-out, innovative, and by-the-numbers approach **Lange Financial Group** takes to retirement and estate planning. But, can your team also help me develop the best plan for me and more importantly, *implement that plan*?

If you too would like more personalized financial help and advice, you may want to have us develop and implement a masterplan by placing a minimum of one million dollars of your investable assets under management (AUM) with Lange Financial Group and team.

We use the tax-saving strategies presented in this book—including Roth IRA conversions (especially after COVID-19), gifting, **Lange's Cascading Beneficiary Plan**, life insurance, charitable trusts, and asset allocation with low-cost enhanced index funds and gifting—to keep your legacy wealth in your family's hands ... and out of Uncle Sam's. All 100% legal, so it won't raise an eyebrow at the IRS.

As far as actually managing your assets, we partner with top money managers, two of whom invest your money in what we consider the best set of enhanced index funds on the planet: Dimensional Funds from **Dimensional Fund Advisors**.

We work with clients who are interested in having at least $1 million of their investable assets managed by us and our partner on an ongoing basis.

To see if you qualify, I urge you to call Lange Financial Group toll-free today at **1-800-387-1129** or go to **page 175** at the back of the book to schedule a FREE initial consultation via phone or Zoom conference. That way, you can meet with us virtually while staying safe and sound in your own home.

There's no charge for the initial consultation or the advice. And no risk or obligation of any kind. The only way you can lose is by not taking advantage of this free offer!

13

Asset Location and How You Should Invest Different Assets in Different Tax Environments

Location, location, location…

I don't usually write about investments and asset allocation. The model that our firm uses for our assets-under-management clients is that our firm "runs the numbers" and develops short and long-term strategies for our clients. Then, one of our strategic partners manage the investments. We charge one combined fee that is generally 1% or less and the money manager and I split the fee. Accordingly, I usually let the money managers write about investments and asset allocation.

We will spare you a basic discussion of asset allocation but do want to bring up a less familiar but extremely critical aspect of managing investments, especially after the SECURE Act—*asset location.* Two of our strategic partners used the concept of asset location in their practices before the SECURE Act and recognize the added importance of asset location after the SECURE Act. They actually have a similar approach to asset location. It is also not a coincidence that the majority of their investments are in index funds (technically enhanced index funds) known as Dimensional Funds from Dimensional Fund Advisors (DFA).

One of our strategic partners, Buckingham Strategic Wealth, and its Pittsburgh Wealth Advisor Adam Yofan, apply an extremely useful strategy when they invest money for a client. They practice asset location to describe which investments should be held in which types of accounts.

Advice from Adam Yofan at Buckingham Strategic Wealth

Given the current tax law—which not only taxes dividends at a lower rate than bond and CD income, but also provides for a step-up in cost basis— equities should generally be held in taxable accounts.

Conversely, fixed income is best held in retirement accounts like traditional IRAs and 401(k)s. Asset classes which have historically demonstrated the highest dimensions of returns (small cap, value, international and emerging markets) are best held in Roth IRA accounts where they most likely have the longest investment time horizon.

Remember: It's not what you earn, it's what you earn *after taxes and expenses*. Since distributions from retirement accounts such IRAs and 401(k)s are taxed at ordinary income rates (the highest tax rates), you'd be well served to develop an asset location and asset distribution plan, rather than just focusing on asset allocation without regard to asset location.

Half of the deaths on Mt. Everest occur on the way down. Remember, the goal isn't to just ascend; it is to ascend and make it back down alive. Depending on your situation, you can no longer just focus on the accumulation of assets. This accumulation focus should not be (1) the end game, nor (2) done without considering the tax impact of the distribution of the assets during your retirement years. It is crucial to develop a spend-down strategy.

A *Spend Down* strategy employs a variety of tactics: Roth Conversion, asset location, Social Security strategy, how much money you can afford to spend and give, as well a strategy for charitable giving if applicable. It also takes your investments—the actual mutual funds, bonds, and stocks you own—into consideration when developing the strategy.

The other strategy that Adam recommends and implements is tax-loss harvesting (see Chapter 7). For the *Mathematics of Asset Location*, consult Appendix C of Larry Swedroe and Kevin Grogan's book, **Your Complete Guide to a Successful and Secure Retirement**.

Our partnership with Buckingham Strategic Wealth—with 35 offices nationwide delivers 1+1=3 value to our clients. They use evidence-based investing as a foundation for their investment philosophy. They have a copyrighted document for the Spend Down process that takes you through the rest of your life. Their goals are to get you the highest risk adjusted return, after-costs and taxes, and to minimize your taxes and your children's inheritance taxes.

The passage of the SECURE Act makes the tax strategies that are discussed in this book and intelligent asset allocation with a special sensitivity to asset location critically important.

Advice from P.J. DiNuzzo of DiNuzzo Wealth Management

The following material comes from another one of our strategic partners, P.J. DiNuzzo of DiNuzzo Wealth Management. The focus of Table 13.1 below is maximizing your after-tax retirement income.

TABLE 13.1
Asset Location
Potential Benefits: Maximize After-Tax Returns

TAXABLE ACCOUNTS (Individual, Joint)	TAX-DEFERRED ACCOUNTS (IRAs)	TAX-EXEMPT ACCOUNTS (Roth IRAs)
Tax-Managed U.S Large	1-Year Fixed Income	Emerging Markets
Tax-Managed U.S Large Value	2-Year Global Fixed Income	Emerging Markets Small
Tax-Managed U.S Small	Short-Term Government Fixed Income	Emerging Markets Value
Tax-Managed U.S Small Value	5-Year Global Fixed Income	International Small Value
Tax-Managed U.S International Large Value	Total Bond Market Fixed Income	International Small
	REITs	
	Commodities	
(Typically Tax-Managed Equity Asset Classes)	*(Asset Classes, mostly bonds, which produce the highest taxable distributions)*	*(Asset Classes with the highest expected rate of return)*

When we look at the three broad account types from left to right you see taxable accounts followed by tax-deferred accounts, and finally tax-exempt accounts. Taxable accounts are typically individual or joint accounts that we refer to as "after-tax dollars." Tax-deferred would normally contain IRAs, 401(k)s, 403(b)s, etc. And, tax-exempt accounts would typically contain Roth IRAs.

In taxable accounts, we want to hold growth assets that have inherent tax-management or tax-aware characteristics. As you can see, funds that we have available through DFA include:

US Large Cap, US Large Value, US Small Cap, US Small Value, and International Large Value, and/or DFA core funds.

Tax-deferred/IRA accounts would typically contain all of our bond funds, and REITs (Real Estate Investment Trusts) asset classes.

Finally, our Roth IRAs would typically hold our highest expected growth with Emerging Markets, Emerging Markets Small, Emerging Markets Value, International Small Value, and International Small.

We are all familiar with the philosophy of asset allocation and diversifying our investments across numerous asset classes. Asset location addresses this question: within our portfolios, are there any accounts in which we can rearrange the investments to better maximize our long-term, after-tax wealth accumulation?

In Table 13.1, equity asset classes eligible for preferential capital gains treatments would be allocated to your taxable brokerage accounts, while bonds/fixed income accounts that generate ongoing ordinary pay are best placed in your IRAs/retirement accounts. Placing equity asset classes, in some cases, into IRAs is unfavorable *because it converts desirable long-term capital gains rates on their growth into ordinary income treatment.*

The *asset location* decisions I am discussing for equity asset classes are highly sensitive to tax-efficiency, and how much dividend income and annual turnover we anticipate in the portfolio. They need to be analyzed on a case-by-case basis.

When considering expected return, tax type, and efficiency, it is advisable to rank our asset classes on an asset location "priority list." Our goal, if it is a good fit, is to place the highest return/efficient investments on one end of our spectrum and the highest return/inefficient investments at the other end.

Once our asset location priority list has been established, we can implement an outside-in approach where the highest return efficient investments are biased toward the taxable brokerage account and the highest return inefficient investments are biased toward the IRA/retirement accounts. By using an outside-in approach, we can attempt to assure that the highest priority investment with the greatest wealth impact will be placed in the proper account(s). Research has indicated that the potential portfolio return benefit of optimal asset location is at approximately 0.10%–0.25% per year.

The comprehensive benefit of optimal asset location decisions is, in reality, difficult to measure, because it depends on what we measure against. It is difficult to project what we may have done in the absence of these additional location decisions. The benefit of asset location also varies depending on the scope of accounts available, and their underlying assets. If you have exclusively taxable accounts, or exclusively IRA accounts there are no asset location benefits available, because we have no options for separate locations.

In conclusion, asset location represents a potential "free lunch" opportunity to maximize long-term wealth growth throughout our individual portfolios by properly implementing tax-efficient strategies.

You must also remember that asset location is a hybrid methodology that results in your various asset location account types having materially different performances. Challenges we have encountered regarding asset location strategies are when members of a household are uncomfortable with the varying performance and underperformance of one spouse's account *vs.* another even though it may be in the best interest of the entire household. The overall hybrid portfolio must carefully consider how to trade all of these accounts in tax-efficient harmony. Rebalancing challenges also emerge if there are insufficient assets in specific account types and how to address this obstacle must be agreed upon before initiating this process.

Investors have two primary aversions: losing money and paying taxes. While we can't control periodic market declines, we can assuage them through diversification and rebalancing. Similarly, although we can't ensure that you will never pay taxes, they can potentially be minimized through asset location optimization, tax lot identification, tax loss harvesting, capital gain harvesting, Roth IRA conversions, and "income smoothing"(tax bracket management). These are the significant tax management strategies that can potentially save you money and add significant value. Through education and quantification, we can get excited about saving money regarding taxes. Strategies for tax-aware portfolio management include but are not limited to:

1. *Asset Location Optimization:* Current taxes may be reduced by shifting ordinary income-producing bonds from taxable accounts to IRAs. Future taxes may be reduced by shifting appreciating securities to taxable accounts (where gains can be taxed at capital gains rates) from IRAs (where gains would be taxed at ordinary rates). Future taxes may be avoided permanently by holding highly appreciated securities in Roth IRAs.

2. *Tax Lot Identification:* Capital gains may be minimized during the rebalancing process by choosing high-cost lots. Although clients with capital loss carryovers might not notice the savings in the current year, tax lot identification can help to preserve the loss carryovers for use when rebalancing gains are unavoidable.

3. *Tax Loss Harvesting:* Tax loss harvesting seeks to recognize losses by selling loss positions solely for tax purposes. Tax loss harvesting produces capital losses, or "deferred tax assets," that can be carried forward indefinitely until used up, thereby offsetting future gains realized from rebalancing (both short term and long term) or more typically annual capital gain distributions.

4. *Capital Gain Harvesting:* Can potentially save investors substantial amounts of capital gain taxes primarily by harvesting gains in current years when future tax rates are expected to be higher. Our primary "sweet spot" for this strategy is the time after a client has retired and before they initiate IRA Required Minimum Distributions (RMDs) at age 72 (formerly age 70½). Harvesting gains in low income years is very powerful.

5. *Bracket Management:* This is another tax savings strategy which I also refer to as "income smoothing." We use income smoothing to obtain the maximum benefit of tax rate arbitrage. I want to reduce taxable income in high income years by maximizing available deductions and then shift income into lower income years. Secondly, I want to increase income in low income years by deferring deductions and increasing taxable income to fill up the lower brackets.

6. *Roth IRA Conversions:* These have a number of advantages over Traditional IRAs. Roth IRAs can lower overall taxable long-term income, offer tax-free growth rather than tax-deferred, have no Required Minimum Distribution (RMD) at age 72 and benefit from tax-free withdrawals for beneficiaries after the death of the owner. During our client's "sweet spot" years we often perform a strategic mix of capital gain harvesting and Roth IRA conversions.

KEY IDEAS

- Both asset allocation and asset location need to be considered to increase returns as safely as possible.
- Tax efficient assets should be invested in taxable accounts.
- Tax inefficient assets should be invested in IRAs or Roth IRAs.

Claim Your FREE DVD:

For over a decade, thousands of investors have profited by attending live **Lange Financial** workshops on trusts, estate planning, tax-saving strategies, and retirement planning.

Now that our live events have been suspended for the duration of the COVID-19 pandemic, we are offering you our newest, FREE DVD:

How to Stop the SECURE Act from Taking up to 1/3 of your IRA and Retirement Plans
(includes a special introduction about COVID-19 and CARES)

There will be overlap between the content of this book and the DVD. But I would like to stress that learning new material is significantly reinforced through repetition and by covering the material through different mediums. So, what you might miss from reading, you might pick up by hearing Jim talk about it!

This DVD gives you the most important tax-saving ideas and strategies from our most recent live financial workshops filmed in February 2020 and updated after COVID-19 and CARES from the comfort and safety of your own home!

To claim your FREE **Best of Lange Financial Workshops DVD**, just call us toll-free **1-800-387-1129** today. There's no charge for the DVD. And no obligation of any kind.

14

More is Better: The Benefits of Combined Strategies

"The whole is greater than the sum of its parts."

— **Aristotle**

In the real world, the best response to defend your family from the dreaded SECURE Act does not merely involve one strategy or one "answer." We almost always recommend a combination of strategies to get the best result for you and your family.

One advantage that we have is that we look at things from a strategic standpoint, a legal standpoint, an investment standpoint, and a tax standpoint. We have CPAs, estate attorneys, wealth advisors all working as a multi-disciplined unified team on the client's behalf.

It is also much better for a client who often gets conflicting advice from his CPA and his attorney, wealth advisor, etc. and must decide who to follow.

In the previous chapters, I showed you how Roth IRA conversions, Lange's Cascading Beneficiary Plan (LCBP), life insurance, low-cost enhanced index funds, asset location, and other strategies can be used individually in your retirement and estate plan to benefit your heirs. This chapter is going to show you that by combining two or more of these strategies, you can create even greater wealth for not only for you and your spouse, but for your entire family.

The practice of combining different strategies forms the cornerstone for most of our client recommendations. We have long been fans of combining Roth IRA conversions, optimizing Social Security strategies, investing in low-cost index

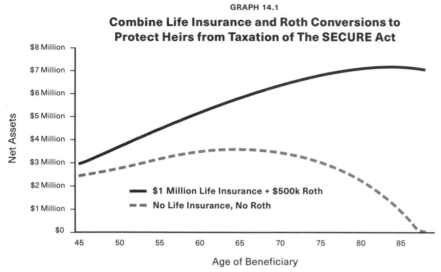

GRAPH 14.1

Combine Life Insurance and Roth Conversions to Protect Heirs from Taxation of The SECURE Act

Please see detailed assumptions in the Appendix.

funds, gifting, and using our favorite estate plan, Lange's Cascading Beneficiary Plan, for many, if not most, married couples who have children only from that marriage (we have other solutions for blended families and same-sex couples). We also combine those strategies with low-cost index (or technically enhanced index) investments using the asset location techniques discussed in Chapter 13.

This chapter examines different combinations of Roth IRA conversions and life insurance.

Combine Roth IRA Conversions and Life Insurance

Graph 14.1 above literally blew me away when I saw it. It seemed too good to be true. The United States has enacted laws that provide enormous rewards for implementing tax-savvy strategies. In previous chapters, we examined the individual benefits of Roth IRA conversions and life insurance, two examples of paying taxes now in return for tax-free growth. The graph above quantifies the benefits of combining Roth IRA conversions (done over several years) and life insurance.

This graph compares two families with identical resources. One family makes a series of Roth IRA conversions and buys life insurance. The other family neither make any Roth IRA conversions nor buys life insurance. The graph shows the trajectory of wealth over the life of the child. The child of the family who

In the real world, the best response to defend your family from the dreaded SECURE Act does not merely involve one strategy or one "answer." We almost always recommend a combination of strategies to get the best result for you and your family.

made the optimal series of Roth IRA conversions and bought life insurance has $7 million when he is in his eighties and the child of the family that neither bought life insurance nor did Roth IRA conversions is broke at the same point in time.

Though in this particular example we combine life insurance and Roth IRA conversions, we usually arrive at the best solution by combining a number of different strategies after "running the numbers." One of the reasons that running the numbers is so hard is that the person running the numbers has to decide which strategies to run and how to combine different strategies. Then even if you know which strategies you are going to combine, the next questions are, "How much of each? How big of a Roth IRA conversion should you make and when?" The same with life insurance and many of these calculations are syner-

gistic meaning that what you do with one variable will have an impact on a different variable, but potentially using both strategies in concert will confer more advantages than using both strategies separately.

The other thing I should mention is that the insurance product in this analysis is a Second-to-Die policy. We are currently looking at using First-to-Die policies and then a Roth IRA conversion after the first death. Unfortunately, we will not have time to do our analysis before this book goes to press.

That said, which type of life insurance and how much to convert to a Roth and when, though extremely important, are secondary to the point of this chapter. The combination of Roth IRA conversions and life insurance is a powerful combination.

Another combination that would make a lot of sense is to include gifting as part of your strategy. Please see Chapter 12 for several types of gifts I recommend.

If our time to analyze more combination strategies and your attention span allowed, we could present an array of successful strategy combination plans. As you can see, there is an enormous difference between optimal and mediocre planning. But this is a huge opportunity to protect yourselves and your heirs and give them a lifetime of financial security. Please consider a combination of strategies to have the biggest impact for yourself and your family.

KEY IDEAS

- Roth IRA conversions, Lange's Cascading Beneficiary Plan (LCBP), charitable remainder trusts, gifting, low-cost enhanced index funds and life insurance can be used individually in your estate plan to benefit your heirs.

  By combining two or more of these strategies, you can create an even greater financial dynasty that will benefit your heirs for generations to come.

- There is a phenomenal difference between optimal and mediocre planning. Strive for optimal planning.

Appendix

The assumptions used in the graphs presented in this book are as follows:

Graph 0.1 Impact of the SECURE Act

1. Child inherits $1 million IRA at age 45 and earns salary of $100,000 annually increasing at 3.5%.
2. Child retires at age 67 and receives $40,000 in Social Security income annually.
3. Rate of return is 7%.
4. Expenses are $90,000 and increases by 3.5% annually.
5. Inherited IRA annual distributions of $147,000.

Graph 0.2 Optimizing Roth IRA Conversions and Social Security

1. $1.1 million in after-tax savings at age 62.
2. 6% rate of return.
3. 3.5% rate of inflation.
4. $50,000 Roth conversions.
5. Spend $75,000 annually.

Graph 1.1 Tax Deferred Savings to Build Your Wealth

1. 7% rate of return.
2. Annual salary to age 67 was $100,000.
3. Social Security at age 67 was $30,000 + spousal $15,000.
4. Annual contributions to retirement plans was $12,000.
5. Annual spending was $80,000; $70,000 after retirement.

Graph 1.2 Spend the Right Money First

1. Investor retires at age 65 with $1.1 million in qualified retirement accounts and $300,000 in after-tax accounts.
2. Assumes annual Social Security income of $25,000 + spousal of $12,500.
3. 25% ordinary tax rates.
4. Beginning annual spending of $90,000; adjusted for inflation annually by 3.5%.
5. 7% rate of return.

Table 2.1 Old Law for IRA Distributions

1. $1,000,000 inherited at age 45.
2. 7% rate of return.
3. 3.5% rate of inflation.

Table 2.2 IRA Distributed Under the SECURE Act

1. $1,000,000 inherited at age 45.
2. 7% rate of return.
3. Annual distributions of $142,500 with balance fully distributed within 10 years.

Graph 3.1 Impact of the SECURE Act –10 Year Distribution

1. Child inherits $1 million IRA (adjusted to purchasing power) at age 45 and earns salary of $100,000 annually increasing at 3.5%.
2. Child retires at age 67 and receives $40,000 in Social Security income annually.
3. Rate of return is 7%.
4. Expenses are $90,000 and increases by 3.5% annually.
5. Inherited IRA annual distributions of $147,000.

Graph 3.2 Grandchild Inherits IRA

1. Grandchild inherits the IRA at age 11 and pays college tuition of $60,000 for four years from proceeds of IRA.
2. During his working years, he earns $80,000 increased annually at 3.5%.
3. The grandchild retires at age 67 and receives $40,000 in Social Security income annually.
4. Expenses are $80,000 and are adjusted by 3.5% annually.
5. Rate of return is 7%.

Graph 6.1 Original IRA Owner After Roth Conversions

1. 7% rate of return.
2. 3.5% rate of inflation.
3. Inflation adjusted dollars.
4. Owner is in 24% tax bracket after age 65.
5. Roth Case: Annual $100,000 Roth conversions for 7 years.
6. Owner has Traditional IRA of $500,000 at age 65.
7. Roth Case: Owner has $125,000 in after-tax assets at age 65.
8. Owner dies at age 85.
9. Owner is better off by $124,399 at death.

Graph 6.2 Child Inherits Roth IRA *vs.* Traditional IRA after The SECURE Act

1. 7% rate of return.
2. 3.5 rate of inflation.
3. Inflation adjusted dollars.
4. Child's wages are $75,000 annually.
5. Child's Social Security at FRA is $30,000 annually.
6. Child's annual expenses are $80,000.
7. Roth Case: Annual $100,000 Roth conversions for 7 years.
8. Parent has Traditional IRA of $500,000 at age 65.
9. Parent die as age 85.

Graph 8.1 Income from a Trust *vs.* IRA Stretched 10 Years

1. 80-year-old parent dies with $1,000,000 IRA & $100,000 cash.
2. 7% rate of return.
3. 3.5% inflation on income and expenses.
4. Child 48 when parent dies.
5. Annual distributions from Inherited IRA $143,000 for 10 years – 32% tax bracket.
6. Total income distributed from IRA, $1,421,399.
7. Total income distributed from CRUT, $1,946,227.
8. Child's wages $100,000 to age 65.
9. Child's Social Security at FRA, $27,000.
10. Child's annual living expenses $90,000.

Graph 12.1 Life Insurance Makes the Difference for This Beneficiary

1. Rate of return 7%.
2. Rate of inflation 3.5%.
3. $1 million life insurance policy.
4. Parents pay $22,000 annual premium on Second-to-Die policy at age 62 forward.
5. Parents die at age 85.
6. At age 66, parents have IRA balance of $1.5million and after-tax savings of $500,000.
7. Parent's combined Social Security at FRA is $52,500.
8. Parent's annual spending is $90,000.
9. Child's wages are $60,000 annually.

Graph 12.1 Life Insurance Makes the Difference for This Beneficiary
(continued)

10. Child retires at age 60.
11. Child's Social Security at age 62 is $15,000.
12. Child's spending is $120,000 annually.
13. Reported in actual dollars.

Graph 14.1 Combine Life Insurance & Roth Conversions to Protect Heirs from Taxation of The SECURE Act

1. Planning parents do five $100,000 Roth conversions.
2. Both parents die at age 85.
3. Child inherits balance of all accounts at age 45.
4. Child lost his savings and retirement plan in divorce.
5. Unmarried child retires at age 60.
6. Unmarried child collects $15,000 in Social Security at age 62, COLAs at 3.0%.
7. Unmarried child spends $120,000 annually.
8. Numbers are in actual dollars.
9. Rate of return 7%.
10. Rate of inflation 3.5%.

Please note, rates of return are not representative of any particular investment or portfolio of investments and cannot be guaranteed. Portfolios holding securities are subject to risk, including the potential for loss of principal. Actual returns will fluctuate.

Why are IRA Owners from All Over the Country Coming to a Small Western PA Office for Advice?

If you're like most IRA and retirement plan owners, you would enjoy enormous benefits by developing and following a true financial masterplan. And now, with the SECURE Act, followed by COVID-19, and the CARES Act, the urgency to develop a *personalized* masterplan is greater than ever.

A personalized masterplan incorporates retirement and estate planning objectives, tax reduction strategies, and investment expertise. But it is also critical to take your personal values, goals, dreams, and comfort level into consideration.

You may enjoy unexpected benefits from working with the appropriate trusted advisor to develop a personalized masterplan. For example, if you have a strong sense of family, a masterplan could include taking your entire family on a vacation every year. These shared memories of your family gatherings will help strengthen a family bond and be a non-financial facet of your legacy. Many of our clients are now taking their families on vacations and using their money to buy experiences, but only after they are confident that they have a long-term plan ensuring sufficient funds.

Don't get me wrong. Developing the perfect long-term Roth IRA conversion plan that saves hundreds of thousands of dollars in taxes is great too. But shouldn't you get both types of perspectives from your trusted advisor?

That combination of head and heart was simply unavailable under one roof, until now. That's why savvy IRA owners from all over the country are flocking to our elite team of CPAs, estate attorneys, and money managers.

We can help you add substantial safety to your legacy in these turbulent times, minimize your tax liability, help you use your money to realize your goals for yourself and your family, and make the dream of generational wealth a reality.

One critical component of developing a masterplan is *running the numbers.* "Running the numbers" is our shorthand for testing a variety of strategies to see which strategy, or more likely which combination of strategies, will work best for you and your family. We are confident that we use the best combination of software programs available for this analysis, but it is really the seasoned experience, and skill of the CPA/number runner that makes this process so valuable.

We provide you with our analysis projecting the outcomes from different planning/taxation scenarios. What we don't give you is 70 pages of computer-generated mumbo jumbo. Our projections are clearly summarized in a few pages outlining which scenarios seem best for your situation and why. We also give you the spreadsheets to see how we arrived at our conclusions. Ultimately, you get to choose your path, but we are guiding you through the…entire process which empowers you to make better decisions. Our process is quite unique and requires highly skilled CPAs, the same CPAs who helped with the quantitative analysis in this book. Because we would never be able to find enough CPAs qualified to handle this level of work, we will never scale and become a huge company, but that is okay with us.

A Haphazard Approach to Planning Undermines Your Future— This is No Time to Wing It

Most IRA and retirement plan owners do not have articulated plans backed up by "running the numbers." What is more probable, is that you have a "collection of decisions" all of which made sense at the time they were made. Sound familiar? But upon detailed analysis, those unconnected decisions usually end up either costing you money in the long run from lost opportunities or worse, leave you vulnerable to unforeseen hazards.

When you started working, you may have consulted with someone to determine which retirement plan options were available to you and how and what to invest. When kids entered the picture, you may have had an attorney draft wills and trusts. You may also have met an insurance salesman and bought some life insurance. Down the line, you invested in stocks, bonds, or financial products outside of your retirement plan. Maybe you hired a CPA who, when asked, gave you limited tax advice. Maybe you did some leg work about Roth IRA conversions, perhaps even reading one of my articles or books, and you converted some of your IRAs to Roth IRAs.

Each decision probably made sense at that time, but they were not part of an *integrated* plan. The sum of the parts does not add up to something greater than the whole. This disconnected process doesn't capitalize on opportunities for tax savings or optimize your retirement plan and/or your legacy plan. Worse, after the SECURE Act and COVID-19, this mode of operation may have left your wealth vulnerable.

Are You a Nail to Someone's Hammer?

Unfortunately, many providers are like a hammer and everyone they meet is a nail. If you sell life insurance, it seems every prospective client needs a large whole-life insurance product as well as a long-term care policy. (I am not particularly a fan of traditional whole-life insurance or traditional long-term care insurance.)

If you are an attorney, everyone needs wills and trusts. And, since you essentially know only a handful of plans, you pick a plan from among the most common estate planning forms that seems to be the best fit for your client.

If you are a CPA, you are likely an excellent historian that accurately reports income from the prior year, but that doesn't make you a tax strategist. If you are a financial advisor, you are likely trying to get the highest return with the least risk. You may have seven or ten sample portfolios and you try to squeeze each client into one of those portfolios. Or worse, you may recommend financial products that often provide the "advisor" with a commission, especially if you do not hold a fiduciary responsibility to your client.

Multiple providers, multiple strategies, no integration. They each talk to you but not to each other. If this sounds familiar, don't blame yourself. Join the crowd. But it does not have to be that way.

When you choose to work with us, we commit to looking at your entire financial and personal picture. We and our joint venture partners work closely together to develop a specific masterplan for you. The left hand knows what the right hand is doing. The head and the heart work in unison.

Our team is familiar with the principles of this book, because we wrote it and have applied them for many years, even before the SECURE Act was passed into law. So, instead of a disorganized and scattered approach, every component of your wealth is integrated into a clear, strategic Financial Masterplan.

You may have a mindset similar to many of our clients. If you are married, no matter how much money you have, you still want to ensure that neither of you will ever run out of money or be forced to reduce your spending, even if the market takes a terrible hit. You want to protect your surviving spouse. You want to take advantage of every legal method to reduce taxes. You want to get the most out of your money while you are alive, and hope to pass on whatever is left in a tax-efficient manner. *But, do you have an optimal plan for doing that?*

The Lange Edge: A Truly Integrated Long-Term Financial Masterplan

When we "run the numbers" and project scenarios for your financial future, we quantify *what you have* and *what you could have* using different strategies. Incidentally, you are in the room, either in person or these days virtually, when we do much of the work. You are not only in the room but are an integral part of the process.

You know how and why we arrive at the recommendations we make for you. You can interject your own "what if" scenarios. We typically narrow the possibilities to a few choices and then ultimately you decide which options best fit your needs and comfort level.

On the topic of comfort...

One of our primary objectives is to provide our clients with financial peace of mind—we want you to sleep well at night. So, in addition to passing the numbers test, our strategies must also pass the stomach test. In other words, can you stand the solution? Often the best solution does push your comfort level, and we may indeed push your comfort level, but you are the boss, we are just the advisors.

Here is an example. It would probably pass the math test, but maybe not the stomach test. Let's say that the following factors suggest a Roth IRA conversion:

- The market is down.
- Your income is down because there is no Required Minimum Distribution this year or maybe you are younger than 72 and don't have a RMD now, but you will soon.
- You are married filing jointly now, but will likely file single after one spouse passes, increasing your tax rate.
- You think taxes in general will go up.
- You don't want to put more money in the market but are concerned with long-term taxation for you and your family.

These factors would, in theory, favor a Roth conversion. Let's even assume that we run the numbers and find that making a $200,000 Roth IRA conversion in 2020 costing $48,000 in taxes is the mathematically best answer. But, let's assume you can't bear to write a check to the IRS for $48,000, but $25,000 would be acceptable. That's fine. We can adapt. The $200,000 solution might not pass the stomach test for you. Sleeping well at night is more important than getting the quantitatively ideal solution.

Deep strategic analysis will persuade you that *there is a better way* to realize your hopes and aspirations. If you have ever tried making financial projections with Excel or other spreadsheets, you will be amazed by how comprehensive and revealing ours are. We have the advantage of knowing and using the best software and, more critically, the skill of our CPAs running the numbers. When we think we have the best financial masterplan, we double check our results by recreating your tax return with our preferred solution to give us and you additional reassurance that we picked the best path.

Finally, we are objective advisors looking at your situation with fresh eyes. I have changed people's lives by asking questions that seemed obvious to me but which the client had never considered. The right questions have opened new possibilities and new opportunities.

One question that frequently sparks interesting discussions and unexpected conclusions is, "If money wasn't a factor, would you continue working?" And, depending on the individual's circumstances, the financial analysis might support the following recommendation:

> "If you want to keep working, work. If you want to retire, retire. The difference in the money isn't that important in your situation. But the choice could have a huge impact on your quality of life."

Lange CPAs, estate attorneys, and our affiliated money managers work as a team to optimize individualized plans and strategies for your benefit. Notice the emphasis on "team." Our firm is driven by collaboration. It is what sets us apart from other estate planning and financial firms. Our CPA firm "runs the numbers," our law firm prepares wills and trusts[8], we review plans annually, and we work in concert with respected low-cost investment advisors who manage the money. Our proprietary quantitative analysis provides definitive answers to questions like these, and more:

1. How much money can you afford to spend without worrying about running out of money?

---

8 Preparing wills, trusts, and IRA beneficiary designations is only available for Pennsylvania residents. Although we cannot draft wills and trusts for out of state clients, *we can review a client's wills and trusts* and then work with local attorneys to implement the legal strategies we think will work best for the client.

2. Should you, and if so, how much and when should you convert from your IRA to a Roth IRA?

3. Does gifting make sense and if so, in what form, how much, and when?

4. What is your best Social Security strategy?

5. Whose name or names should be on a particular asset?

6. What is the best way to provide for your heirs?

7. What is the best estate plan for your situation?

8. What is the best way to provide for the causes/charities you support?

9. What are the most tax-savvy solutions for you and your family?

What comes to light in this process can be surprising. You may have many more options to grow and use your wealth and protect yourself and your family than you ever imagined. You may also be more vulnerable to extreme taxation than you realized.

We can also help answer questions with facts, not suppositions. Perhaps you think you can't afford to both maintain your existing house and buy a second home in a warmer climate. We can run the numbers and find out. You might discover it is financially feasible to become snowbirds and get the best of both worlds. Observations like these have been life-changing and liberating for our clients.

Some have found they have enough money to retire immediately. Others prefer to continue working, but on their own terms. One professor who found financial freedom through our process stated it colorfully and with passion: "I'm not going to quit tomorrow, but I'm not going to take any #%! from the chair anymore." She ended up in much happier working conditions because she no longer feared the financial consequences of asking for (and getting) what she wanted both in terms of money and working conditions.

We Concentrate on Working with IRA and Retirement Plan Owners

We don't try to be everything to everybody. Some firms aggressively court any prospective client who has a certain amount of investable assets. We, on the other hand, choose to focus on providing comprehensive integrated tax, financial and estate planning services to a specific type of client.

We provide the most value to clients who have the majority of their investable assets in their IRAs and retirement plans. This type of portfolio requires radically different strategies than a portfolio where IRAs and retirement plans play a much smaller role. Americans who have more money in their IRAs and retirement plans than they do outside of those plans have unique tax, retirement, estate, and financial planning needs. They can take advantage of unique opportunities, but they are also at risk of falling into costly quagmires. We understand those needs. In fact, we have concentrated our research, analysis, and practice in planning for IRA and retirement-plan-heavy clients for the last twenty-five years.

I wrote the first peer-reviewed article on Roth IRA conversions in 1997, even before the Roth IRA conversion law became effective in 1998. In that same article, we advocated for the flexible estate plan that is now known as Lange's Cascading Beneficiary Plan—still the ideal estate plan for many retired and married IRA and retirement plan owners.

The plan gained huge attention and has since been referenced in *The Wall Street Journal* multiple times, *Financial Planning* magazine, and many other places. Just Google "Cascading Beneficiary Plan" and you can see it is all over, and most of the sources point back to us. Ask us about it if you take advantage of our *Retire Secure Consultation* (see page 175).

We predicted the "death of the stretch IRA" five years ago, and I have written two previous books on the topic. We were implementing and recommending "work-arounds" for our clients to compensate for the then looming threat that we accurately predicted would become law.

Over the past three decades we have developed and honed proven solutions to address the needs of clients with large IRAs and retirement plans, and serving those clients is what we do best.

Who Manages the Money?

Lange Financial Group, LLC does not manage money. We focus on what we do best: number-crunching and tax and legal strategies to guide your decision making. We leave the money managing to our joint venture partners so they can do what they do best.

We work closely with an elite group of top investment advisory firms that bring the same kind of dedication and concentration to their field as we do to ours: DiNuzzo Wealth Management, Fort Pitt Capital Group, and Buckingham Strategic Wealth.

The magic happens when we work with one of our joint-venture partners to focus on achieving the best outcome for our clients.

DiNuzzo Wealth Management

Since 1989, DiNuzzo Wealth Management has specialized in Wealth Planning, Financial Planning, and Investment Management. Regarding Investment Management, DiNuzzo's core belief is based upon "Efficient Market Theory" and accessing its many benefits through indexing. DiNuzzo invests in the capital markets based on enhanced indexing; specifically in institutional, low-cost mutual funds developed by market leader Dimensional Fund Advisors (DFA).

DFA's genesis, history, and continued advancements are rooted in academia, not Wall Street or Main Street. Their fundamental tenets are empirical and evidence based. Historically, access to invest in DFA's institutional mutual funds was reserved for major institutions. DiNuzzo was one of the first 100 Registered Investment Advisor (RIA) Investment Managers in the U.S. to receive permission, and remains among a limited group, approved by DFA to offer Dimensional Funds to individual investors like you.

DiNuzzo performs the Wealth Planning and Investment Management, while Lange Financial advises clients in retirement planning estate planning, Roth IRA conversions, Social Security, and other tax-saving strategies—all 100% legal—and we combine forces to work in the best interest of our mutual clients.

DiNuzzo places an equal emphasis on their fiduciary process and financial education. In particular, they share my belief that an informed and knowledgeable client sets the foundation for a long, successful client/advisor relationship.

I have seen DiNuzzo turn down opportunities because the prospective client was not a good fit. And I have seen DiNuzzo morph a big opportunity into a modest opportunity because it was the right thing to do for the client.

DiNuzzo and their team pride themselves on relationship management and as such, strive for frequent communication with our mutual clients. I believe they have always been extremely pro-active getting in front of our clients, but they have been particularly diligent with client communication since COVID-19 hit us all so hard.

DiNuzzo Wealth Management also has an excellent strategy for protecting pre-retirement and retired investors with what they refer to as a *Glide Path*. Yes, if the market has a thirty-year bull market after you retire, you will not do as well by following DiNuzzo's glidepath. But, if the markets are volatile and/or take a major downturn, as they did recently, and they take many years to recover, there will always be food on the table, a shelter over your head, gas in the car, and a little money for Saturday night.

I never worry that a client that I refer to DiNuzzo will end up broke because they didn't sufficiently plan for a potential downturn. That said, DiNuzzo additionally presents a compelling case against too much money in fixed income (bonds and cash) because of the lost opportunity danger of taxes and inflation.

Fort Pitt Capital Group

We also have a similar joint venture arrangement with the active money managers at Fort Pitt Capital Group.

Fort Pitt communicates its investment strategies for each Lange client openly, clearly, and simply. They do not engage in flagrant "market timing." Their team designs investment portfolios to be flexible enough to capitalize on good prospects when it makes sense, yet stable enough to preserve your legacy for the long-term.

Fort Pitt investment advisors manage your money with thoughtfulness and analytical rigor. Through the market's ups and downs, Fort Pitt sticks to the plan, and doesn't chase fads of the industry. They are always ready to explain their decisions and work with clients to establish a clear understanding of objectives and outcomes.

Fort Pitt can help you increase your wealth with a diversified investment portfolio that's focused on growing your money for the long term. As a fiduciary, your financial security is their top priority.

Buckingham Strategic Wealth

Buckingham Strategic Wealth, a $35 billion dollar company, is an independent wealth management firm with headquarters in St. Louis and 35 (and growing) offices throughout the country, including an office in Pittsburgh.

Like DiNuzzo, Buckingham has Dimensional Funds—managed by Dimensional Fund Advisors (DFA)—at the core of the portfolios they manage. Buckingham also offers a selection of additional investment options that are not available through our other joint venture partners. Just recently I received this email from Adam Yofan, "The bond market is more screwed up than the stock market. Yesterday rates for AAA munis (municipal bonds) were paying TWICE the CD rate. After tax, obviously much more." This sounds like smart advisors looking for opportunities for their clients to me.

They have a dedicated team that buys and sells approximately $2 billion in bonds and FDIC insured CDs annually on behalf of their clients. As a fiduciary,

Buckingham is always obligated to put client interests first. For fixed income, this means no hidden mark ups or commissions when buying bonds or CDs. By buying individual bonds or CDs, this also means that their clients may be able to avoid costly mutual fund expenses by not using bond funds.

When it comes to CDs, Buckingham uses FDIC insured Brokered CDs, which may offer better rates and/or terms than the rates you can get at your local bank.

Buckingham has a proprietary process to guide your finances through the rest of your life. They offer 40 activities that help minimize taxes, maximize cash flow, and protect your assets. They also "run the numbers" but in a much different way and for different purposes than the way our firm "runs the numbers." Their "running the numbers" which utilizes Monte Carlo, is more investment orientated than our process. Their process is a perfect complement to our strategic "running the numbers."

The recommendations they make are based on decades of peer-reviewed financial research and contemporary market analysis. Their long-view combined with current research gives them the judgement and power to make optimized and strategic investments—they know how to invest.

The cornerstone of Buckingham's approach is their evidence-based investment philosophy, which is built on a deep understanding of how to best capture the returns of the financial markets. Their approach is based on facts and evidence, not opinions. They are not swayed by "flavor of the month" speculation. I have met with the CEO and most of the top people at Buckingham, and I could not have been more impressed. Most of the advisors are CPAs and CFPs and their background is technical, not sales. The true fiduciary culture is obvious with each individual that you meet.

Perhaps even more important than the people at the top of corporate is the advisor who works with you. The advisor most clients will work with is Adam Yofan, who heads up the Pittsburgh office. Prior to heading the Pittsburgh office of Buckingham Strategic Wealth, Adam served as President of Alpern Wealth Management for 13 years. Before that, he was a financial advisor for Smith Barney for five years, and a senior manager for Deloitte & Touche for 12 years. He has earned his Personal Financial Specialist and Certified Public Accountant designations. The PFS designation is only available to CPAs who meet extra requirements, which helps make him so rare. In sum, he is a top-notch advisor working for an excellent true fiduciary company that offers our favorite set of investments on the planet.

How Our Joint Venture Partnerships Work to Your Benefit

The arrangement we have with all three money management firms is essentially the same. Our joint venture/partner money-management firm develops an investment plan, and with the right hand knowing what the left hand is doing, our team develops a comprehensive retirement and estate plan. Then we help you—now our mutual client—implement the overarching plan.

But our involvement doesn't end there. All good plans need to be modified and adjusted due to changing circumstances—portfolios increase and decrease because of market conditions, tax laws change, children marry, grandchildren are born, and divorces happen. That's why you'll meet at least once annually to update your masterplan with the person from our firm who helped develop it. Of course, these days these meetings are virtual.

You'll also meet with the money management firm's team on a more regular basis to review portfolio performance and integrate the strategies that our firm develops. Even better, all of these integrated and value-added services you receive from us and our joint venture partner firm are included as part of the management fee you pay to our partner firm.

What Advantages Does Our Arrangement Offer You?

When you become a client of Lange Financial Group, LLC, you benefit from the *integrated* experience of our world-class financial professionals—all of whom have different but complementary expertise. In essence, you are getting what we think are the best retirement, estate planning, and money management strategies available anywhere for a combined fee that is likely less than you would be paying for the sole services of a money manager.

You get the benefit of our award-winning retirement and estate planning strategies on an ongoing basis and premiere integrated money management services all for *one* reasonable fee. *That sounds great, but how much does this cost?*

You pay one fee (depending on how much money is invested) that is typically between 50 basis points (one-half of one percent) and 1% of the money we manage. It is the identical fee that you would pay any one of our money managers if you had not met us first. The money manager and our firm then split the fee. Imagine getting an extremely valuable strategic plan that is updated every year and integrated money management services for a total of one percent or potentially less than 1%, depending on how much money we manage per year.

The Next Step

We have put our hearts and souls into this book and hope you find it a valuable resource. We also hope that it inspires you to consider some of the charitable techniques mentioned in this book, to help raise a billion dollars for charity.

Most importantly, I hope reading the book has motivated you to take action. I heard an interesting definition of "learning" recently, which is that learning leads to "a change in behavior through experience, instruction, or study." So, by that definition if you found the information in this book interesting, but you aren't ready to take any action, then you haven't actually "learned" anything. That may be a bit harsh, but my larger point is that if you learn something and don't take action, especially when it comes to your family's long-term security, you haven't accomplished anything.

If you are a do-it-yourselfer and would rather have a root canal than pay an advisor a fee for services, I genuinely hope you found value in this book. But again, don't just read it and think "that was great information, maybe I'll do something about it later." Because "later" usually means "never." Take action now. Make the changes that signify learning.

If, on the other hand, you see the value of working with me and a team that will implement the best strategies in this book, you might appreciate our total value proposition.

If so, you now stand at a critical crossroads for yourself and your family. You can do nothing, which is not really doing nothing; it is making an active decision not to pursue financial protection from the devastating new tax law and realize the opportunities that could literally change your family's financial destiny.

You can say "I'll think about it," but people who say that usually get distracted with other concerns.

Or, you can take action to improve your situation. If you think it would be a good fit to work with us, you would be well served to take advantage of the *Retire Secure Initial Consultation* (which at this point would be with me). Just check the first box on the following form. We also offer other choices, but the best choice for right-fit clients is the *Retire Secure Initial Consultation.*

Yes, Jim, I want your help running the numbers to develop a personalized masterplan that will also protect my IRA and other retirement accounts from the disastrous consequences of the new SECURE Act.

In particular, I'm interested in *(check all that apply)*:

❑ Retire Secure Initial Consultation[9]

❑ Personalized Financial Masterplan[10]

❑ Estate Planning (PA residents only)—*including drafting of wills, trusts and beneficiary designations of IRAs and retirement plans.*

❑ Free "Retire Secure" workshop DVDs

❑ Free Lange Financial Group Online Newsletter—*including book updates*

❑ Other *(describe)* _____

Name _____

Address _____

City _____ State _____ Zip _____

Phone _____ Email _____

4 Easy Ways to Respond:

By Phone: Call toll-free **1-800-387-1129** and **ask for Alice**

By Fax: Fax this completed form to **412-521-2285**

Online: Visit **https://paytaxeslater.com/RetireSecureConsultation**

By Mail: Alice Davis
Lange Financial Group
2200 Murray Avenue Pittsburgh, PA 15217

....

9 We do not offer this *Retire Secure Initial Consultation* to everyone. To qualify for this free consultation, which is now held by phone or Zoom, you must have $1 million or more in investable assets that you would consider placing under management with Lange Financial Group—assuming you like our retirement planning and tax-saving strategies as well as our money manager and his process and investment options. We develop financial masterplans for all our assets-under-management clients and update those plans annually, and the cost of those services is covered by the management fee.

10 We help you develop a financial masterplan for $7,500, potentially more for $10 million and larger estates, but you handle the investments and implementation of the plan. It is a one-time fee and one-time service. There is also a good chance we will run out of capacity for these plans as helping our assets under management clients is our first priority. We may raise the price of stand-alone financial master plans if we are overwhelmed with work which is a likely possibility.

About the Author

James Lange, CPA, Attorney, and registered investment advisor is a nationally recognized IRA, 401(k), and retirement plan distribution expert. Jim deeply resents provisions in the SECURE Act that trigger massive taxes for hard-working IRA and retirement plan owners and their families.

He sees huge gaps in strategic IRA and retirement planning that are unaddressed by most CPAs, attorneys, and financial advisors. Jim is passionate about protecting the financial security of his clients and readers and their families—this book is a result of that passion.

Jim has never been this excited about the possibility that one of his books could help raise a billion dollars for charity! The math clearly shows that, for many IRA owners, leaving your IRAs to a charitable remainder trust could result in much more money for your family, more money for your favorite charities, and significantly less for the IRS. The goal of helping families and directing a billion dollars to charity is attainable. It has inspired Jim to work harder to get his message out more than any of his previous seven best-selling books. (See praise for Jim's previous books on page xv.)

Jim is the principal member of **Lange Legal Group, LLC, Lange Accounting Group, LLC** and **Lange Financial Group, LLC.** Jim's companies serve over 1,600 clients. Jim has presented hundreds of workshops for taxpayers and financial professionals throughout the country, and his workshops consistently get the highest ratings.

Just prior to the coronavirus pandemic, Jim held three capacity-audience workshops presenting his best strategies to defend retirement plan owners from the worst tax consequences of the SECURE Act. *(Fortunately, the workshops were videotaped. Please see page 153 for more information on how to request the DVDs.)*

His small Western PA practice is capturing the attention of IRA and retirement plan owners nationwide. With 35 years of experience, Jim and his staff offer unbeatable recommendations combining legal, tax, and investment expertise all under one roof. Their unique combination of services helps IRA and retirement plan owners develop a personalized masterplan for growing and protecting their wealth. And now, with the SECURE Act, followed by COVID-19, and the CARES Act, the urgency to develop a *personalized* masterplan is greater than ever.

Jim also developed **Lange's Cascading Beneficiary Plan (LCBP)**, which is widely regarded as the gold standard of estate planning for many married IRA and retirement plan owners. His office has administered hundreds of estates whose families have benefitted from these plans.

His ideas have been endorsed 36 times in *The Wall Street Journal.*

Jim sincerely hopes you will act to follow the strategies in this book to change the future for yourself and your family.

Jim lives in Pittsburgh, in the home he grew up in, with his wife, Cindy, and their daughter, Erica. When Jim is not devising new strategies for retirees to save taxes and accumulate wealth (which is most of the time), he enjoys bicycling, hiking, skiing, and traveling with his family. Jim also plays chess and bridge both online and with his friends.

Notes:

Notes: